HPBooks

Microwaving With An International Flair

by Susan Brown Draudt

ANOTHER BEST SELLING VOLUME FROM HPBOOKS
Photography: deGennaro Associates
Food Styling: Carol Peterson

HPBooks
A division of Price Stern Sloan, Inc.
360 North La Cienega Boulevard
Los Angeles, California 90048

Printed in U.S.A.

9 8 7 6 5 4 3 2 1

Cover Photo: Shellfish Stew, page 82.

Library of Congress Cataloging-in-Publication Data
Draudt, Susan Brown.
Microwaving with an international flair.

1. Microwave cookery. 2. Cookery, International.
I. Title.
TX832.D725 1988 641.5'882 88-21325
ISBN 0-89586-686-2

Contents

Susan Brown Draudt

Susan Brown Draudt's favorite appliance is the microwave oven. Her busy family life led to the development of these delicious and quick-to-prepare microwave recipes. A professional home economist, Susan's wide experience includes development of consumer education materials, product demonstrations and food photography. She also teaches cooking classes (in Southern California) and develops new recipes. She is the author of three HPBooks cookbooks; *Food Processor Cookery*, *30-Minute Meals* and *Microwaving for 1 or 2*. A native Californian, Susan, husband Dennis and children Danielle and Michael now reside in Massachusetts.

Introduction

Foods from around the world have always held an intrigue for good cooks. With the recent increase in wonderful ethnic restaurants and the wide availability of international fruits, vegetables, herbs and spices in supermarkets, more and more cooks have begun preparing foreign dishes.

Up to now recipes with a foreign flair have usually been interpreted as complicated and time consuming. Luckily, the microwave oven knows no boundary lines. I have found that what the microwave oven does for American food, it does beautifully for all types of cuisines. Quick cooking times combined with fresh flavors and exotic aromas give foreign dishes prepared in the microwave oven even more appeal.

Chinese and French cuisines are historically considered the two great cuisines of the world. Their contributions of preparation techniques and innovative ingredients have given the world a wonderful array of foods. The food of any country reflects its political and cultural history. The various dishes native to each country were originally determined by the ingredients available as well as the sophistication of their cultures. Over the centuries invading soldiers carried their own native dishes with them as they conquered new territory. The combination of a country's original cuisine with these new dishes and foods created an even more varied cuisine.

Due to the crossover of tastes and ingredients from one country to another, eating the cuisine from different countries might not be as foreign as you would expect. If you like the spiciness of Szechuan food, you probably will enjoy the same spiciness found in Mexican or Thai food. While English food is usually considered very bland, in fact a mild French custard called *Creme Anglaise* translates to English Cream, they do have some wonderfully spicy chutneys from their colonial days in India.

Every effort has been made to make these recipes uncomplicated to prepare using ingredients widely available. As there is a wide variation in preparation methods and cultural differences for many recipes, some liberty has been taken to make the recipes understandable and easy to accomplish.

Confucius is credited with saying "Food is the first happiness." which is true in any country.

Menus
LATIN AMERICAN BRUNCH
MEXICO
Sangria
(Fruited Wine Punch)
BRAZIL
Salada de Tomate
(Tomato Salad)
SPAIN
Tortilla a la Paisana
(Country Omelet)
Warm Flour Tortillas and Butter
PUERTO RICO
Cafe Frio
(Cold Coffee)
EUROPEAN CONTINENTAL PICNIC
ENGLAND
Shandy
(English Beverage)
SPAIN
Almejas Frias
(Cold Mussels)
FRANCE
Poulet au Montrachet
(Chicken with Goat Cheese)
FRANCE
Ratatouille
(Eggplant, Onions & Peppers)
French Bread Baugettes with Sweet Butter
ITALY
Macedonia Di Frutta
(Marinated Apricots & Figs)

ORIENTAL DINNER
CHINA
Sui Mai
(Steamed Dumplings)
INDONESIA
Sayur Goreng
(Cabbage with Chicken)
SINGAPORE
Kway Teow
(Curried Noodles)
CHINA
Fun Tsen Tien Niu Ro
(Steamed Beef with Sweet Potatoes)
Fluffly White Rice
PHILLIPINES
Coconut Pudding
SCANDANAVIAN BUFFET
SCANDANAVIA
Julsallad
(Christmas Eve Salad)
DENMARK
Bloomkaal
(Cauliflower & Shrimp Salad)
FINLAND
Lanttulaatikko
(Turnip Casserole)
SWEDEN
Fiskrulader med Citronsas
(Rolled Fish with Lemon Sauce)
DENMARK
Rødgrød med Fløde
Fruit Pudding with Cream
Coffee

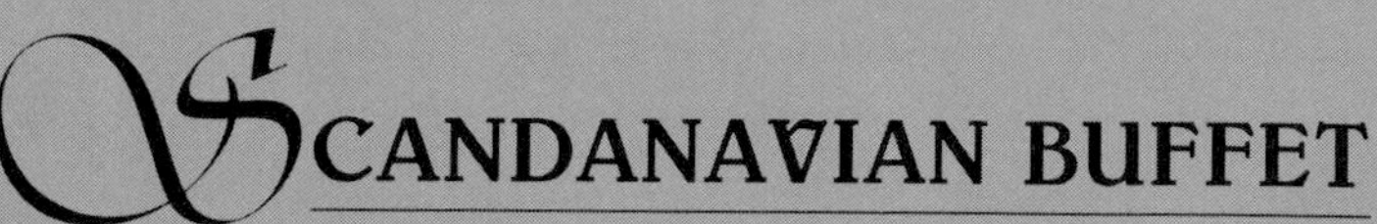

SCANDANAVIAN BUFFET

Christmas Eve Salad

Califlower & Shrimp Salad

Turnip Casserole

Rolled Fish with Lemon Sauce

Fruit Pudding with Cream

Coffee

Christmas Eve Salad

Julsallad *Scandanavia*

No Christmas smörgasbord *would be complete without a Jul ham, Christmas Eve Salad and an assortment of appetizers with a rich rice pudding for dessert.*

1 (.25-oz.) envelope unflavored gelatin
1/4 cup sugar
1 cup water
2 tablespoons fresh lemon juice
1 cup apple juice
1 large cooking apple, cored, diced
1 cup diced pickled beets
1 cup finely shredded red cabbage
Lettuce leaves

In a medium-size microwave-safe bowl, combine gelatin, sugar, water and lemon juice. Let stand 5 minutes to soften gelatin. Microwave on 100% (HIGH) 3 minutes or until water starts to boil. Stir until gelatin and sugar dissolve. Stir in apple juice. Chill until mixture begins to thicken. Fold in apple, pickled beets and red cabbage. Pour into a 1-quart mold. Refrigerate about 4 hours or until set or overnight. Line a serving plate with lettuce leaves and unmold salad onto lettuce leaves. Makes 6 servings.

Cauliflower & Shrimp Salad

Bloomkaal — Denmark

If fresh cauliflower is not available, you can substitute two (ten-ounce) packages of frozen cauliflower.

1 small head cauliflower
1/2 cup mayonnaise
1 tablespoon Dijon-style mustard
2 tablespoons chopped green onions
1/2 lb. bay shrimp, cooked, peeled, deveined

Cut cauliflower in bite-size flowerets. Place in a medium-size microwave-safe bowl. Cover tightly. Microwave on 100% (HIGH) 5 to 7 minutes or until tender. Rinse under cold running water to cool. Drain well. To make dressing, combine mayonnaise, mustard and green onion in a small bowl. In a serving bowl, toss cauliflower and shrimp with dressing. Makes 4 to 6 servings.

Turnip Casserole

Lanttulaatikko — Finland

This casserole can be made with rutabagas, turnips, potatoes or a combination of these vegetables. It can also be prepared ahead of time and microwaved or reheated before serving.

6 or 7 medium-size turnips, peeled, diced
1/4 cup fresh bread crumbs
1/4 cup whipping cream or milk
2 eggs, beaten
1/2 teaspoon salt
1/4 teaspoon ground allspice
1/4 teaspoon ground nutmeg
3 tablespoons butter or margarine

Place turnips in a medium-size microwave-safe bowl. Cover tightly. Microwave on 100% (HIGH) 8 minutes or until tender. Let stand, covered, 10 minutes. Mash turnips and mix in bread crumbs, cream, eggs, salt, allspice and nutmeg. Spoon mixture into a 1-1/2-quart microwave-safe dish. Smooth out top and dot with butter. Microwave on 70% (MEDIUM-HIGH) 10 to 12 minutes or until heated through. Makes 6 servings.

NOTE
If refrigerating casserole before microwaving, add 4 to 5 minutes to microwaving time.

Rolled Fish with Lemon Sauce

Fiskrulader med Citronsas — *Sweden*

All of Scandanavia is well known for its seafood. Fishing is one of their largest industries, so you know there must be lots of great seafood recipes.

4 (6-oz.) white fish fillets
1 (8-oz.) bottled clam juice
2 tablespoons butter or margarine, softened
2 tablespoons all-purpose flour
Salt and black pepper to taste
1 tablespoon fresh lemon juice
6 ozs. cooked peeled deveined small bay shrimp

Roll up fillets, jelly-roll style. If necessary, secure with a wooden pick. Place in a small flat-bottom microwave-safe dish. Pour clam juice over fish. Cover tightly. Microwave on 100% (HIGH) 6 to 8 minutes or until fish is opaque. Let stand, covered, 5 minutes. Remove fish to a serving dish; cover to keep warm. To prepare sauce, In a small microwave-safe bowl, combine butter and flour. Microwave on 100% (HIGH) 30 seconds. Stir to mix well. Stir butter mixture into liquid in dish. Microwave on 100% (HIGH) 2 to 3 minutes or until mixture starts to thicken. Season with salt and pepper. Stir in lemon juice and shrimp. Microwave on 100% (HIGH) 1 minute or just until shrimp is heated. Pour sauce over fish. Makes 4 servings.

Fruit Pudding With Cream

Rødgrød med Fløde — *Denmark*

Anyone who loves berries will certainly enjoy this dessert. Because it is thickened with cornstarch, it will tend to weep a little. Don't make it too far in advance of serving.

3 cups fresh or frozen strawberries, red currants, blackberries or raspberries, thawed if frozen, drained, juice reserved
About 2 cups water or reserved berry juice
3/4 cup sugar
1/3 cup plus 2 tablespoons cornstarch
Whipping cream

In a large microwave-safe bowl, combine fruit and 2 cups of water or reserved berry juice. Microwave on 100% (HIGH) about 10 minutes or until mixture comes to a boil, then microwave 5 minutes more. Strain through a very fine sieve into a 4-cup measure. If needed, add additional water or juice to make 4 cups puree. In a 1-cup measure, dissolve cornstarch in 1/4 cup of water or juice. Stir into fruit puree. Microwave on 100% (HIGH) 8 minutes or until mixture begins to bubble. Whisk to blend well and prevent lumps. Microwave on 100% (HIGH) 5 minutes more, stirring 2 or 3 times. If desired, pour into a serving bowl. Let stand until room temperature. Refrigerate until set, about 4 hours or overnight. Spoon into individual serving dishes and serve with cream. Makes 8 servings.

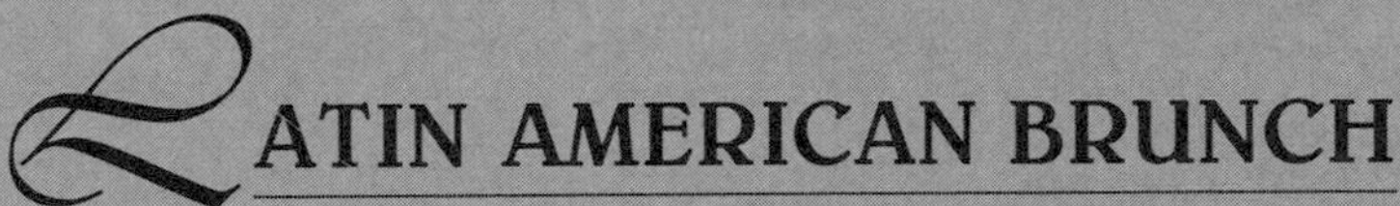

LATIN AMERICAN BRUNCH

Fruited Wine Punch
Tomato Salad
Country Omlet
Cold Coffee

Fruited Wine Punch *(Photo on page 35)*

Sangria — *Spain*

My first introduction to sangria was in Spain, and as a teenager I thought it was terrific. Several years later, I still find this citrus and wine combination refreshing.

1/2 cup water
3/4 cup sugar
Peel 1 orange
Peel 1 lemon
Juice 2 oranges
1 (750-ml.) bottle dry red wine
3 cups club soda
Lime slices and orange peel to garnish

To make sugar syrup, in a large microwave-safe bowl, combine water, sugar and orange and lemon peels. Microwave on 100% (HIGH) 3 to 4 minutes. Cool to room temperature. Remove and discard peel. In a large pitcher, combine sugar syrup, orange juice, wine and club soda. Pour into iced glasses. Garnish with lime slices and orange peel. Makes about 8 servings.

Cold Coffee

Cafe Frio — *Puerto Rico*

1 cup water
1 teaspon instant coffee granules
Crushed ice
2 scoops vanilla ice cream
2 ozs. light rum

In a 1-cup glass measure, microwave water on 100% (HIGH) 2 minutes. Stir in coffee granules and let stand until cold. Fill a 14-ounce glass half full of ice. Add ice cream and rum. Fill glass with cold coffee and stir. Makes 1 serving.

Tomato Salad

Salada de Tomate — *Brazil*

Serve this salad hot or let the chili mixture cool to room temperature before combining it with the lettuce. You can make this salad hotter by adding more of the hot-pepper sauce.

1 medium-size head lettuce
2 large tomatoes, diced
1/3 cup olive oil
1/3 cup vegetable oil
1 medium-size onion, diced
1/2 cup chopped yellow bell pepper
1/2 cup chopped red bell pepper
1/2 cup chopped green bell pepper
1/2 cup chopped fresh cilantro
1/3 cup fresh lemon juice
1 clove garlic, minced
1/2 teaspoon hot-pepper sauce, if desired

Tear lettuce in bite-size pieces. Place in a salad bowl with tomatoes. In a microwave-safe bowl, combine olive and vegetable oils, onion, yellow, red and green bell peppers, cilantro, lemon juice, garlic and hot-pepper sauce, if desired. Microwave on 100% (HIGH) 6 to 7 minutes or until bell peppers are tender, stirring twice during cooking. Pour hot mixture over lettuce, toss and serve immediately. Makes 6 servings.

Country Omelet

Tortilla a la Paisana — *Spain*

Both Spain and France claim to have invented the omelet. Spain claims a Spanish chef introduced it to the court of Louis XIV. France feels it was invented in a Carthusian Monastery and taken to Spain by the Monks.

1/4 cup olive oil
4 or 5 fresh green beans, cut in 1/2-inch lengths
1/4 cup frozen green peas
1/2 cup diced cooked potato
1/2 cup diced cooked ham
2 tablespoons tomato paste
6 eggs, beaten

In a large microwave-safe bowl, combine 2 tablespoons of olive oil, green beans, green peas, potato, ham and tomato paste. Microwave on 100% (HIGH) 3 to 4 minutes or just until hot, stirring after 2 minutes of cooking. Set aside. Add remaining olive oil to an 8-inch round microwave-safe cake dish. Swirl to coat bottom of dish. (Olive oil is more for flavor than for its nonstick properties.) Pour in beaten eggs. Microwave on 100% (HIGH) 3 minutes. Gently stir, bringing cooked outer edges to center. Microwave on 100% (HIGH) 2 to 3 minutes more or until just set. Omelet should be lightly moist on top. Spoon vegetable mixture down center of omelet. Fold both sides over center. Slide out onto a serving dish. Cut in slices to serve. Makes 3 to 4 servings.

EUROPEAN CONTINENTAL PICNIC

Shandy
Cold Mussels
Chicken with Goat Cheese
Eggplant, Onions & Peppers
Marinated Apricots & Figs

Shandy

England

To make this English pub favorite, combine your favorite beer and lemon syrup. Try it on a hot summer day.

3/4 cup water
1 cup beer

Lemon Syrup:
1/2 cup water
1 cup sugar
1 cup fresh lemon juice

Prepare Lemon Syrup. In a large glass, mix 1/3 cup of Lemon Syrup and water. Pour in beer. Makes 1 serving.

Lemon Syrup:
In a 4-cup glass measure, combine water and sugar. Microwave on 100% (HIGH) 3 minutes or until sugar dissolves, stirring several times during cooking. Cool to room temperature. Stir in lemon juice. Refrigerate tightly covered. Makes about 2 cups.

Cold Mussels

Almejas Frias *Spain*

Spain is well known for its fresh shellfish. This mussel dish could be served as an entree on a hot day or as an appetizer.

24 mussels, cleaned
2 tablespoons fresh lemon juice
1/4 cup plus 2 tablespoons olive oil
Freshly ground black pepper to taste

Place mussels in a single layer in a large deep microwave-safe dish. Cover tightly. Microwave on 100% (HIGH) 3 to 5 minutes or until mussels open. Discard any mussels that do not open. Remove top shell. In a small bowl, mix lemon juice and olive oil. Spoon over mussels. Season with pepper. Refrigerate to chill at least 1 hour or overnight before serving. Makes 4 servings.

Chicken with Goat Cheese

Poulet au Montrachet *France*

Montrachet *is a mild cheese made from goats milk. Goat cheese has been popular for centuries internationally, but only recently has gained popularity in the United States.*

2 (4-oz.) boneless skinned chicken breasts, pounded 1/4-inch thick
3 tablespoons butter or margarine, softened
1/2 teaspoon dried leaf tarragon, crushed
1 teaspoon paprika
1 tablespoon dry white wine
2 ozs. Montrachet goat cheese, cut in 4 slices
6 thin slices tomato

In a medium-size flat-bottom microwave-safe dish, combine butter, tarragon, paprika and wine. Microwave on 100% (HIGH) 30 seconds or until butter melts. Place chicken in butter mixture, turning to coat each side. Cover loosely with waxed paper. Microwave on 100% (HIGH) 2 minutes. Turn chicken over. Microwave on 100% (HIGH) 1 to 2 minutes more or until chicken is cooked through. Alternate 3 tomato slices with 2 cheese slices on each piece of chicken. Cover loosely with waxed paper. Microwave on 100% (HIGH) 1 minute or until cheese melts. Serve warm or chilled. Makes 2 servings.

Eggplant, Onions & Peppers

Ratatouille *France*

Ratatouille, *pronounced Rah-tah-twee, is a combination of vegetables, usually containing eggplant. But any concoction of squash, tomatoes and various colored bell peppers work well together. This can be served as a side dish to an entree or cold as an appetizer.*

1/4 cup olive oil
1 medium-size onion, thinly sliced
1 medium-size eggplant, diced
2 medium-size bell peppers, thinly sliced
1 clove garlic, minced
3 medium-size tomatoes, seeds removed, diced
1 tablespoon finely chopped fresh basil
1/4 teaspoon freshly ground black pepper

Combine all ingredients in a large deep microwave-safe casserole dish. Toss to coat all vegetables with oil. Cover tightly. Microwave on 100% (HIGH) 8 to 10 minutes or until vegetables are tender. Let stand, covered, 10 minutes before serving. Makes 4 servings.

Marinated Apricots & Figs *(Photo on page 145)*

Macedonia Di Frutta *Italy*

Any combination of dried fruits works well in this not-so-sweet dessert. Let the fruits marinate overnight to develop the flavor and tenderize.

8 ozs. dried figs, cut in half lengthwise
4 ozs. dried apricots
1 cup fresh orange juice
1/2 teaspoon shredded lemon peel
3/4 cup ricotta cheese
1/8 teaspoon vanilla extract
Dash grated nutmeg
Toasted sliced almonds to garnish

Place figs, apricots, orange juice and lemon peel in a medium-size microwave-safe bowl. Cover tightly. Microwave on 100% (HIGH) 5 to 6 minutes. Without removing cover, gently shake bowl to "stir" fruit. Let stand, covered, until room temperature. Refrigerate overnight or at least 4 hours to chill completely. In a small bowl, combine ricotta cheese, vanilla and nutmeg. Refrigerate until ready to serve. Spoon fruit and juice into individual dessert bowls. Top each with a dollop of ricotta cheese mixture. Garnish with toasted almonds. Makes 4 servings.

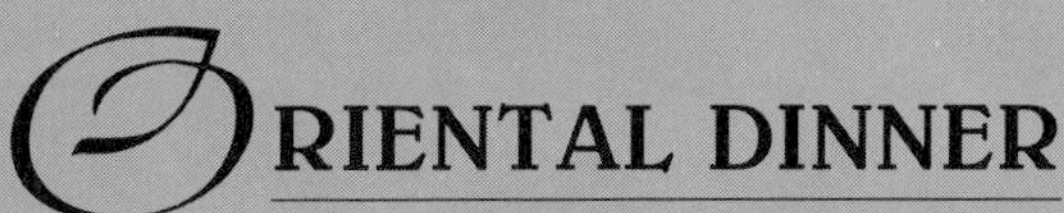

ORIENTAL DINNER

Steamed Dumplings
Cabbage with Chicken
Steamed Beef with Sweet Potatoes
Curried Noodles
Fluffy White Rice
Coconut Pudding

Steamed Dumplings

Sui Mai — *China*

Dim sum is Cantonese for "heart's delight." Snacks and treats served in oriental tea houses can be eaten whenever one's heart so desires! These dumplings can be served as an appetizer or as dim sum *in a large assortment of finger foods.*

12 (3-inch) round or square wonton skins
1/4 lb. ground pork
2 tablespoons finely chopped water chestnuts
3 tablespoons finely chopped bok choy or cabbage
1 tablespoon finely chopped green onion
1/2 teaspoon rice vinegar
1 teaspoon soy sauce
1/4 teaspoon chopped gingerroot
1/2 clove garlic, chopped
2 large bok choy or cabbage leaves

If wonton skins are square, cut in rounds by trimming off corners. In a large bowl, combine ground pork, water chestnuts, bok choy, green onion, vinegar, soy sauce, gingerroot and garlic. Mix well. To shape dumpling, place 1 wonton skin on palm of hand. Spoon 1 rounded tablespoon of meat mixture into center. Cup hand and gently shape wonton skin around meat mixture. Repeat with remaining wonton skins and meat mixture. Flatten bottom of each dumpling. Place bok choy leaves on a serving platter. Cover tightly with plastic wrap. Microwave on 100% (HIGH) 1 minute or until leaves are limp. Place filled dumpings on leaves, spacing evenly. Re-cover and microwave on 100% (HIGH) 5 to 6 minutes or until pork is no longer pink in center. Let stand, covered, 5 minutes. Makes 12 dumplings.

Cabbage with Chicken

Sayur Goreng *Indonesia*

Sayur Groeng *translates to "cabbage fried," but in the microwave oven, it isn't really fried. Use green cabbage if bok choy is not available.*

2 fresh red chili peppers, stem and seeds removed
1 clove garlic
1/2 onion, minced
2 tablespoons vegetable oil
1 (4 oz.) boneless skinned chicken breast, diced
1 small head bok choy or green cabbage, thinly sliced

In a food processor fitted with the metal blade or a blender, process chili peppers, garlic, onion and oil to a puree. Spoon puree into a large microwave-safe bowl. Microwave on 100% (HIGH) 1 minute and 30 seconds or until very hot. Stir in chicken. Cover tightly. Microwave on 100% (HIGH) 1 to 2 minutes or until chicken is tender and coated with puree, stirring twice during cooking. Stir in cabbage. Cover tightly. Microwave on 100% (HIGH) 2 to 3 minutes or just until cabbage is wilted. Toss mixture to mix. Makes 4 servings.

Steamed Beef with Sweet Potatoes

Fun Tsen Tien Niu Ro *China-Szechuan*

The combination of savory flavors are absorbed by the beef so that when it is cooked with the potatoes, the flavors permeate the entire dish.

1 lb. beef tenderloin
2 tablespoons soy sauce
1 teaspoon sugar
1 tablespoon dry sherry
1 teaspoon sesame oil
1 teaspoon finely chopped gingerroot
1/4 teaspoon salt
2 medium-size sweet potatoes, peeled, cut in 1-inch cubes

Slice beef against grain in 1/8-inch-thick slices. In a medium-size bowl, mix soy sauce, sugar, sherry, sesame oil, ginger and salt. Stir in beef. Cover tightly. Refrigerate 30 minutes. Arrange sweet potatoes in bottom of a medium-size flat-bottom microwave-safe dish. Arrange beef on top. Cover tightly. Microwave on 100% (HIGH) 5 minutes. Carefully stir beef so it will cook evenly. Re-cover and microwave on 100% (HIGH) 3 to 5 minutes more or until sweet potatoes are tender. Let stand, covered, 5 minutes. Makes 4 servings.

Curried Noodles

Kway Teow — *Singapore*

This is a one-dish meal, similar to what Americans would call a casserole. Feel free to add bits of cooked beef, pork or chicken.

2 tablespoons vegetable oil
3/4 onion, thinly sliced
1 teaspoon curry powder
2 cups bok choy (Chinese cabbage)
1 cup bean sprouts
3/4 cup chicken stock
1 cup cooked peeled deveined small shrimp
2 tablespoons soy sauce
3 cups cooked rice thread noodles
1 teaspoon toasted seasame seeds
1 tablespoon thinly sliced green onions

In a large deep microwave-safe casserole dish, combine oil, onion and curry powder. Cover tightly. Microwave on 100% (HIGH) 4 minutes. Stir in bok choy, bean sprouts and chicken stock. Re-cover and microwave on 100% (HIGH) 3 to 4 minutes or until bok choy is limp. Mix in shrimp, soy sauce and rice thread noodles. Cover tightly. Microwave on 100% (HIGH) 2 minutes. Stir. Re-cover and microwave on 100% (HIGH) 2 to 3 minutes more or until heated through. Sprinkle with sesame seeds and green onion. Makes 4 servings.

Coconut Pudding

Philippines

The cuisine of the Philippines and Hawaii are so closely intermingled, it's hard to know which country first developed this dessert.

1/3 cup cornstarch
1/4 cup sugar
2 cups milk
1 cup flaked sweetened coconut
1/2 teaspoon vanilla extract

In a medium-size microwave-safe bowl, combine sugar and cornstarch. Stir in milk. Microwave on 100% (HIGH) 6 to 8 minutes or until mixture is smooth and thickened. Stir in coconut and vanilla. Pour into a serving dish. Cover tightly. Refrigerate 4 hours or until well chilled. Makes 6 servings.

Appetizers & Beverages

Hors d'oeuvres around the world are traditionally served at the dining table as a first course. In America we seem to prefer our *hors d'oeuvres* served with wine or a cocktail in the living room, then we proceed to the dining room.

Tapas, the Spanish word for *hors d'oeuvres*, are usually served in the late afternoon at home or in the local bars. They range from something as simple as roasted almonds or olives to an extensive array of sandwiches and seafood. Often an entire meal is made from *tapas* and drinks.

Hors d'oeuvre is a French word meaning a small serving of something savory to whet not dull the appetite. Fresh vegetables lightly cooked and topped with vinaigrette, a slice of a savory tart or *pâté* served with crusty French bread and butter and probably a white wine to drink are typical French appetizers. Excellent quality ingredients, not over garnished and very neatly arranged on the serving plate, are the keys not only to French *hors d'oeuvres* but to presenting wonderful appetizers in any language.

Without a doubt the two most popular beverages world wide are coffee and tea. While neither have any caloric or nutritional value, they do have important culinary and economic value.

The Venetians, it is said, introduced coffee to the Western World. They still take its preparation and service very seriously.

Tea plants were originally grown in China and by the fifth century A.D. tea was an important export. The Dutch with their superior sailing force introduced tea to Europe, but it wasn't very successful. The Germans preferred their beer and the French felt that compared to their strong coffee brews, tea was suitable only for the invalid and old. England embraced tea as it's national drink. An afternoon tea has become an institution, creating a special group of foods to serve with tea—biscuits, finger sandwiches and sweets.

Wine is also a universal beverage. It is used in cooking for flavor, in marinades to add tenderness and as a base for what is called hot mulled wine in America, *glögg* in Scandanavia and *gluhwein* in German. The German translation is "glow wine" and I'm not sure if the wine looks like its glowing from the heat or if your face starts to glow from the wine!

Peanut Sauce

Num Jim Sate — *Thailand*

Thailand cooking has been influenced by its neighbors, China and India. The spices used here are the clue.

1 tablespoon vegetable oil
2 tablespoons finely chopped onion
1/4 teaspoon ground coriander
1/8 teaspoon ground cumin
1/4 cup peanut butter
1/4 cup water

In a small microwave-safe bowl, combine oil, onion, coriander and cumin. Cover tightly. Microwave on 100% (HIGH) 1-1/2 to 2 minutes or until onion is very tender. Stir in peanut butter and water. Re-cover and microwave 1 to 2 minutes more. Stir until very smooth. Serve warm as a dipping sauce. Makes 1/2 cup.

Pickled Eggs

England

Pickled eggs are often found marinating in jars in English pubs and waiting to be eaten!

12 hard-cooked eggs, peeled
3 cups malt or cider vinegar
2 teaspoons ground ginger
2 teaspoons mixed pickling spice
1/3 cup sugar
1 teaspoon whole peppercorns

Place eggs in a large jar or deep bowl. In a 4-cup glass measure, combine vinegar, ginger, pickling spice, sugar and peppercorns. Microwave on 100% (HIGH) 10 to 15 minutes or until mixture comes to a boil; pour over eggs. Cover and refrigerate 3 days to let flavors penetrate eggs. Store in refrigerator up to 2 weeks. Makes 12 eggs.

Pickled Onions

E n g l a n d

Serve these crunchy onions with a hearty sandwich or with an assortment of hors d'oeuvres. Malt vinegar is a mild vinegar sometimes used on English fish and chips.

2 cups malt or cider vinegar
2 tablespoons sugar
1 teaspoon ground ginger
1 tablespoon mixed pickling spice
1 small piece cinnamon stick
1 lb. (about 2-1/2 cups) small white boiling onions, peeled

In a large microwave-safe bowl, combine vinegar, sugar, ginger, pickling spice and cinnamon piece. Microwave on 100% (HIGH) 8 to 10 minutes or until mixture comes to a boil. Add onions and microwave on 100% (HIGH) until mixture comes back to a boil; microwave 4 minutes more. Spoon onions into a sterilized jar and pour vinegar mixture over onions. Cover and refrigerate 5 days before serving. Store in refrigerator up to 2 weeks. Makes 3 cups.

Old English Cheese Crock *(Photo on page 25)*

E n g l a n d

Serve this herbed cheese at room temperature with an assortment of English biscuits or crackers. Most supermarkets carry English biscuits.

1/4 cup whipping cream
1 tablespoon dry sherry
1 teaspoon Worcestershire sauce
1 teaspoon minced green onion
1/8 teaspoon white pepper
1/8 teaspoon dried leaf tarragon
1/8 teaspooon dried leaf thyme
1 teaspoon Dijon-style mustard
1/4 lb. sharp Cheddar cheese, finely shredded (1 cup)
Green onion stems to garnish

In a medium-size microwave-safe bowl, combine whipping cream, sherry, Worcestershire sauce, green onion, white pepper, tarragon and thyme. Microwave on 100% (HIGH) 1 to 1-1/2 minutes or until cream starts to boil. Quickly stir in mustard and cheese. If cheese does not melt to a smooth paste, microwave on 100% (HIGH) 30 seconds and stir. Repeat if necessary. Garnish with green onion stems. Makes about 1 cup.

Shrimp on a Stick

No Ka Oi Pupus — *Hawaii*

Whole large shrimp, heads on, are needed for this recipe. I saw this in Hawaii and was fascinated by the look. It's a real eye catcher!

1 cup rice vinegar
1/2 teaspoon minced gingerroot
1 garlic clove, minced
1/4 cup minced green onion
12 fresh whole large shrimp, legs removed
12 (10-inch) wooden skewers

In a large bowl, combine vinegar, gingerroot, garlic and green onion; stir in shrimp. Refrigerate 1 hour, stirring twice during refrigeration. To thread shrimp on a skewer, lay shrimp on a flat surface, then push in skewer lengthwise from tail to head. Repeat with remaining shrimp and skewers. Place skewers on a microwave-safe serving platter. Cover tightly. Microwave on 100% (HIGH) 4 to 6 minutes or until shrimp shells turn red. Makes 12 appetizers.

Orange Shrimp Kebabs (Photo on page 25)

Camarines Naranjo — *Spain*

Most people think of Italy when olive oil is mentioned, but Spain produces a lovely light oil that blends well for a marinade. You'll need long wooden skewers for this appetizer.

1 lb. fresh medium-size shrimp, peeled
1/2 cup olive oil
1/4 cup white wine vinegar
2 tablespoons fresh orange juice
2 teaspoons freshly grated orange peel
1 garlic clove, minced
1/2 teaspoon red pepper flakes
1/4 teaspoon black pepper
2 medium-size oranges, pared, cut in large pieces
1 (8-oz.) can whole water chestnuts, drained
1/2 small unpeeled cucumber, halved lengthwise, cut in slices
18 pimento-stuffed green olives
18 (10-inch) wooden skewers

Place shrimp in a large flat microwave-safe dish. In a 2-cup measure, combine olive oil, vinegar, orange juice and peel, garlic, red pepper flakes and black pepper; pour over shrimp. Cover tightly. Microwave on 100% (HIGH) 3 minutes. Stir to rearrange shrimp. Re-cover and microwave 2 to 3 minutes more or just until all shrimp are pink. Refrigerate at least 2 hours or overnight. To assemble, thread shrimp, orange pieces, water chestnuts, cucumbers and olives on skewers. Makes 18 appetizers.

Shrimp with Basil Dipping Sauce

U. S. A.

Shrimp served as an appetizer steal the show. Everyone loves them!

2 lbs. fresh medium-size shrimp, shelled, deveined
1/4 cup dry sherry
1-1/2 cups ketchup
1/2 cup fresh basil leaves
3 tablespoons soy sauce
1 tablespoon Worcestershire sauce
Crushed ice

Place shrimp with tails attached in a flat microwave-safe dish. Pour sherry over shrimp. Cover tightly. Microwave on 100% (HIGH) 3 to 5 minutes or until shrimp are pink. Let stand, covered, 5 minutes. Refrigerate until ready to serve. To prepare dipping sauce, process ketchup, basil, soy sauce and Worcestershire sauce in a food processor fitted with the metal blade or a blender to a puree. To serve, arrange chilled shrimp on crushed ice with a bowl of dipping sauce in center. Makes 8 appetizer servings.

Shrimp Satay

Saté Ledang — *Indonesia*

Sate is the shish kebab of the Orient. Chicken, lamb, beef or pork can be substituted for the shrimp. The meat is marinated, then skewered and cooked. Peanut sauce is generally served as a condiment.

1/2 cup coconut milk or regular milk
1 tablespoon soy sauce
1 tablespoon finely minced onion
1/4 teaspoon ground ginger
1 garlic clove, finely minced
1-1/2 lbs. medium-size shrimp, deveined, peeled
8 to 12 wooden skewers
1 recipe Peanut Sauce, page 20

In a large bowl, combine coconut milk, soy sauce, onion, ginger and garlic. Add shrimp; refrigerate 2 hours. Thread shrimp on wooden skewers. Place sate in a flat microwave-safe casserole dish. Cover tightly. Microwave on 100% (HIGH) 4 to 6 minutes or until shrimp turn pink. Serve with Peanut Sauce. Makes 8 to 12 appetizers.

Cheesy Tomato Bread

U. S. A.

The word marinade comes from Spain where it means "to pickle." Early marinades began as simple brines for preserving fish. Today more sophisticated marinades contain a wide variety of herbs, spices and flavorings combined with an oil and acid (lemon juice, vinegar or wine) base. To make this an authentic marinade, you might try a Spanish olive oil.

1/4 cup olive oil
3 tablespoons red wine vinegar
1 teaspoon dried leaf basil
1/2 teaspoon seasoned salt
1/4 teaspoon black pepper
1/4 cup diced red onion
1/2 cup diced tomato
8 thin slices French bread
4 ozs. thinly sliced Swiss cheese
Fresh baby basil leaves to garnish

In a small bowl, whisk olive oil, vinegar, dried basil, seasoned salt and pepper. Stir in onion and tomato. Cover and refrigerate at least 4 hours or overnight. Line a microwave-safe plate with paper towels. Toast bread. Cut cheese slices to fit bread. To assemble, brush toasted bread with marinade. Top each slice of bread with a slice of cheese and 1 tablespoon of onion and tomato mixture. Place on prepared plate. Microwave on 100% (HIGH) 30 to 60 seconds or just until cheese melts. Garnish with basil leaves. Makes 8 appetizers.

Cheese Filled Tortilla

Quesadilla

Mexico

In our family no Mexican meal is complete without a quesadilla to start it off. A quesadilla can easily become a complete meal by adding shredded chicken or beef to the filling. The sour cream and guacamole toppings are a personal preference. If desired, you omit them.

2 large flour tortillas
2 ozs. shredded Monterey Jack cheese (1/2 cup)
2 ozs. shredded Cheddar cheese (1/2 cup)
2 tablespoons diced green chilies
2 tablespoons sliced ripe olives
1 green onion, finely chopped
1/4 cup green chili salsa
1/2 cup dairy sour cream
1/2 cup guacamole

Place 1 tortilla flat on a microwave-safe plate. Sprinkle with cheeses, chilies, olives, green onion and salsa. Top with remaining tortilla. Microwave on 100% (HIGH) 1 to 1-1/2 minutes or until cheese melts. Spread sour cream and guacamole over top. Cut in wedges. Makes 2 to 4 appetizer servings.

Clockwise from top: Cheesy Tomato Bread, above; Old English Cheese Crock, page 21; Orange Shrimp Kebabs, page 22.

Crab & Chili Nachos

Nachos de Jaiba — *Mexico*

Nachos contain ingredients that are distinctively Mexican, like cheese, chilies and salsa. But they are so popular in the West and Southwest of the U.S., it's hard to know to which country this recipe belongs.

2 cups tortilla chips
1/4 lb. Cheddar cheese, shredded (1 cup)
1/2 cup taco sauce or salsa
4 ozs. crab meat
2 tablespoons sliced green onion

Spread tortilla chips on a microwave-safe platter. Sprinkle evenly with cheese. Spoon on taco sauce, crab meat and green onion. Microwave on 100% (HIGH) 1 to 3 minutes or until cheese melts. Makes 2 to 4 appetizer servings.

Cajun Pecans

Southern U. S. A.

Mention the word Cajun and visions of hot spiciness appear. Pecans are grown in the southern part of the U.S. and are usually associated with sweet foods, but they are wonderful with this savory coating.

1 cup pecan halves
1 tablespoon butter or margarine
1/4 teaspoon salt
1/4 teaspoon cayenne pepper

Place all ingredients in a small microwave-safe bowl. Microwave on 100% (HIGH) 2 minutes. Stir to evenly coat all pecans. Microwave on 100% (HIGH) 1 minute more or until you can hear buttered pecans sizzling. Spread pecans on paper towels to drain. Serve slightly warm or at room temperature. Makes 1 cup.

Chicken Liver Pâté

Pâté de Foies de Volailles — *France*

The chicken livers are cut in half to prevent them from popping while cooking. Their high fat content causes them to cook quickly.

1/2 cup unsalted butter
1 medium-size onion, thinly sliced
1 lb. chicken livers, cut in half
1 hard-cooked egg
1 tablespoon brandy
Salt and freshly ground black pepper to taste
Small toast rounds or crackers

Place butter and onion in a flat microwave-safe dish. Microwave on 100% (HIGH) 5 minutes or until onions are well done. Add chicken livers. Cover tightly. Microwave on 100% (HIGH) 2 to 3 minutes or just until chicken livers are done. In a food processor fitted with the metal blade, process chicken liver mixture, egg and brandy just until smooth. Season with salt and pepper. Scrape out into a small terrine. Cover and refrigerate overnight for best flavor. Serve with toast rounds or crackers. Makes about 2 cups.

Small Marinated Fish

Pescaditos en Escabeche — *Spain*

This recipe falls into Spain's food category called entremeses variados—*meaning assorted hors d'oeuvres. It is a hearty and spicy appetizer that stimulates your appetite.*

1-1/2 lbs. mackerel or tuna fillets
3 tablespoons olive oil
2 garlic cloves, mashed
Pinch saffron
1/4 teaspoon ground cumin
1/4 teaspoon ground ginger
1/3 cup cider vinegar
2/3 cup water
1/2 lemon, sliced thinly

Brush fish with olive oil. Cut in 3'' x 2'' pieces. Place fish in a flat microwave-safe casserole dish. Cover tightly. Microwave on 100% (HIGH) 3 to 4 minutes or until fish is no longer translucent. In a small dish, mix garlic, saffron, cumin and ginger. Stir in any remaining olive oil, vinegar and water. Pour over fish. Lay lemon slices on top of fish. Cover and refrigerate overnight. Makes 4 to 6 appetizer servings.

Steamed Clams

Almejas a la Marinera — Spain

This is one of those tapas *(Spanish appetizers) of which you could easily make a whole meal. Mussels are a wonderful substitution for the clams or combine them.*

12 small clams
1 cup dry white wine
1/2 teaspoon freshly ground black pepper

Rinse clams and soak in a large bowl of water 1 hour to clean out sand. Combine wine and pepper in a deep microwave-safe casserole dish large enough to hold clams in a single layer. Drain clams and place in wine. Cover tightly. Microwave on 100% (HIGH) 3 to 5 minutes or until clams open. Discard any that do not open. Let clams cool in wine. Serve with wooden picks. Makes 3 or 4 appetizer servings.

Toasted Almonds

Almendras Rustida — Spain

Toasted almonds are almost always offered when an array of tapas *(Spanish appetizers) are served.*

2 cups water
1 cup unsalted shelled almonds
2 tablespoons olive oil
1/2 teaspoon salt

Place water in a 1-quart microwave-safe bowl or 4-cup glass measure. Microwave on 100% (HIGH) 7 minutes or until water starts to boil. Remove from oven and add almonds. Let stand 2 minutes. Drain off water. Slip off brown almond skin by pinching almonds at 1 end. Return almonds to 1-quart bowl. Microwave on 100% (HIGH) 2 to 4 minutes or until hot, stirring after 1-1/2 minutes. Add olive oil and salt; toss to evenly coat almonds. Spread almonds on paper towels to absorb excess oil. Serve warm or at room temperature. Makes 1 cup.

Cream Cheese & Pepper Relish

Kajmak I Ajvar — Y u g o s l a v i a

Feta cheese is usually associated with Greek cuisine, but historical maps show the Greeks left behind their cuisine preferences as they explored Europe. The bell peppers will peel easily after cooling to room temperature.

2 medium-size red bell peppers
1 medium-size green bell pepper
1/4 cup Italian salad dressing
1 garlic clove, minced
Pinch dried red chilies
1/2 cup butter or margarine, softened
1/4 lb. feta cheese (1 cup)
1 (3-oz.) pkg. cream cheese, softened
Sliced pumpernickel bread

Wrap bell peppers tightly in plastic wrap. Microwave on 100% (HIGH) 6 to 8 minutes or until soft. Let stand until room temperature and peel. Remove stem and seeds and chop bell peppers finely. In a small bowl, combine bell peppers, salad dressing, garlic and chilies. Refrigerate until ready to serve. In a medium-size bowl, combine butter, feta cheese and cream cheese until completely mixed. To serve, invite guests to spread bread with cheese mixture and top with bell peppers. Makes 10 appetizer servings.

Toasted Coconut Strips

Tiritas de Coco — M e x i c o

Coconuts are usually associated with tropical climates. Wide strips of unsweetened coconut (chipped coconut) can be purchased in health food departments or stores. If you have fresh coconut available, use a vegetable peeler to shave off thin strips of the coconut meat.

1 cup chipped coconut

Line a microwave-safe plate with paper towels. Spread coconut in 1 layer on prepared plate. Microwave on 100% (HIGH) 1 to 3 minutes, watching carefully. Coconut should just start to brown, but will burn quickly. Let stand until room temperature to crisp. Makes 1 cup.

Bean Dip

Frijoles Para Sopear — *Mexico*

I first tasted this dip in 1976, thinking it to be a new California concoction using Mexican ingredients. Imagine my surprise when I found a similar recipe in a Mexican cookbook published in the mid-1950's. Packaged tortilla chips were not even known in the U.S. then.

1 (16-oz.) can refried beans
1/2 cup dairy sour cream
1 (1-oz.) envelope dry taco seasoning mix or 1/2 cup salsa
2 to 4 drops hot-pepper sauce
Tortilla chips

Place refried beans in a medium-size microwave-safe bowl. Microwave on 100% (HIGH) 3 minutes. Stir in sour cream, taco seasoning mix and hot-pepper sauce. Microwave on 100% (HIGH) 2 minutes more, then stir. Serve dip warm with tortilla chips. Makes 2 cups.

Hot Anchovy Dip

Bagna Cauda — *Italy*

Hot bath is the English translation of this hot garlic and anchovy-flavored vegetable dip. Any selection of fresh vegetables, cut in bite-size pieces, will work. Even small cubes of French bread on wooden picks make great dippers.

1/2 cup butter
1/2 cup olive oil
1 teaspoon finely chopped garlic
1 (2-oz.) can anchovy fillets, finely chopped
French bread cut in small cubes
Assorted fresh vegetables cut in bite-size pieces

Place butter in a small microwave-safe serving bowl. Microwave on 100% (HIGH) 1 minute or until melted. Stir in olive oil, garlic and anchovies. Microwave on 100% (HIGH) 1 to 2 minutes more or until very hot. Insert wooden picks into bread cubes. Serve bread and fresh vegetables with dip. If mixture cools before guests finish, microwave on 100% (HIGH) 30 to 60 seconds or until very hot. Makes 1 cup.

Snails in Garlic Butter

Escargots à la Bourguignonne *France*

Imported snails in cans can be found in the gourmet section of large supermarkets. They are especially grown for eating. The snail meat is usually canned and packaged with the shells in which to serve. I like to serve this recipe with a good French bread to soak up every drop of the tasty garlic butter.

1 (12-piece) can snails and shells
3 tablespoons butter or margarine
1/2 teaspoon chopped garlic
French bread

Place snail meat, butter and garlic in a microwave-safe pie plate. Cover tightly. Microwave on 100% (HIGH) 2 minutes. Stir to evenly coat snails. Using a fork, stuff 1 snail into each shell. Spoon any remaining butter mixture into shells. Serve on salad-size plates or special snail dishes with French bread. To reheat, microwave 6 snails in their shells on 100% (HIGH) 30 seconds. Makes 3 servings.

Mushrooms in Wine

Champignon à Vin *France*

If the mushrooms are very large, cut them in half or fill them with chunks of fresh tomato tossed with a vinaigrette.

3 tablespoons olive oil
3 tablespoons fresh lemon juice
2 tablespoons finely chopped onion
1 bay leaf
8 ozs. fresh medium-size mushrooms, cleaned

In a flat microwave-safe dish, combine olive oil, lemon juice, onion and bay leaf. Microwave on 100% (HIGH) 2 minutes. Stir in mushrooms. Cover tightly. Microwave on 100% (HIGH) 3 minutes more. Remove bay leaf. Cool to room temperture or chill before serving. Makes 4 servings.

Country Pâté

Pâté Froid — *France*

Pâté comes in two different forms —the classic goose or chicken liver pâté, such as pâté fois gras, *and the country type which is a combination of ground meats, usually resembling a firm meat loaf.*

1/2 lb. bacon
2 tablespoons butter or margarine
1 bunch green onions, chopped
1 lb. lean ground pork
1 lb. ground veal
2 eggs
1/2 lb. chicken livers, chopped
1/2 cup Calvados or apple brandy
3/4 cup fresh bread crumbs
1/3 cup milk
1-1/2 teaspoons salt
1/2 teaspoon ground nutmeg
1/4 teaspoon black pepper

Reserve 3 strips of bacon. Line bottom and sides of a 9'' x 5'' x 3'' microwave-safe loaf pan with remaining bacon. In a large microwave-safe bowl, place butter and green onions. Microwave on 100% (HIGH) 3 minutes or until onions are slightly cooked, stirring once. Combine butter and onions with ground pork and veal, eggs, chicken livers, brandy, bread crumbs, milk, salt, nutmeg and pepper. Pack tightly into prepared pan. Place reserved bacon slices on top. Cover tightly. Place loaf pan in microwave oven on an inverted microwave-safe saucer. Microwave on 100% (HIGH) 10 minutes. Drain and gently press down top. Microwave on 70% (MEDIUM-HIGH) 10 to 15 minutes more or until done. Let stand 10 minutes. Drain off fat and cool to room temperature. Remove from pan. Wrap tightly and refrigerate overnight. To serve, cut in thin slices. Pâté may be frozen for future use. Makes 8 servings.

Cooking Tip:
When cooking or reheating any food, always use less time than called for. It's easy to add more if needed.

Eggs in Gelatin

Oeuffs en Gelée — *France*

Whole eggs in clear unflavored gelatin make a beautiful presentation. Serve these eggs as an appetizer or a salad. Soft boiled eggs can be used; I prefer to hard-cook the eggs. A dollop of good mayonnaise on top is a nice flavor addition.

2 (12-1/2-oz.) cans chicken consomme
2 (.25-oz.) envelopes unflavored gelatin
1/2 cup dry white wine
1 tablespoon tarragon vinegar
12 fresh tarragon leaves
1/4 cup liver pâté or liverwurst
6 hard-cooked eggs, peeled

Measure 1 cup of consumme into a medium-size microwave-safe bowl. Stir in gelatin. Microwave on 100% (HIGH) 3 minutes or just until consomme comes to a boil. Stir until gelatin is completly dissolved. Add remaining consomme, wine and vinegar. Set aside. In a 2-cup glass measure, microwave 1 cup water on 100% (HIGH) 3 minutes or until water reaches a boil. Drop tarragon leaves into boiling water to blanch, then quickly plunge into cold water. Place 6 (6-oz.) oval molds or custard cups in a pan of iced water. Spoon 1 tablespoon of gelatin mixture into each. Let stand about 5 minutes or until set. Arrange 2 tarragon leaves in each mold. Stir pâté until smooth. Using a pastry bag fitted with a small star tip, pipe pâté in small star designs around tarragon leaves. Gently spoon 1 tablespoon of gelatin mixture into each mold, being careful not disturb design of leaves and pâté. Let stand 5 minutes or until gelatin is set. Place 1 egg in each mold. Pour in enough gelatin to cover. Refrigerate molds and any remaining gelatin until set. To unmold, briefly dip molds into hot water and invert on a serving tray. To garnish, chop remaining gelatin finely and sprinkle on serving platter. Makes 6 servings.

Hot Dutch Chocolate

Warme Chocolademelk — *Holland*

The Dutch are well known for their high quality chocolate. This drink combines cocoa powder and chocolate liqueur for an extra good tasting chocolate drink.

3 tablespoons cocoa powder
3 tablespoons sugar
4 cups milk
1/2 cup chocolate liqueur
Whipped cream

In a large microwave-safe bowl, combine cocoa powder, sugar and milk. Microwave on 100% (HIGH) 8 minutes. Stir until chocolate is completely dissolved. Microwave on 100% (HIGH) 2 to 3 minutes more or until hot but not boiling. Stir in chocolate liqueur. Pour into 4 mugs. Top with dollops of whipped cream. Makes 4 servings.

Mexican Hot Chocolate

Chocolate Mexicano — *Mexico*

This is hot chocolate whipped until it froths! Mexicans use a wooden molinillo *to whisk the chocolate; a wire whisk will work as well.*

1/2 oz. sweet chocolate, finely chopped
1 cup milk
Pinch cinnamon
2 (6-inch) pieces cinnamon stick

In a 2-cup glass measure, combine chocolate, milk and cinnamon. Microwave on 100% (HIGH) 2 to 3 minutes or until hot but not boiling. Beat with a whisk until chocolate is dissolved and milk is very foamy. Place cinnamon pieces in hot chocolate. Makes 1 serving.

Eggnog

Rampope — *Mexico*

The method of preparation is the defining point between Mexican eggnog and that familiar to the United States. The cinnamon is steeped in hot milk to give a richer flavor.

4 cups milk
1 cup sugar
1 (3-inch) piece cinnamon stick
10 egg yolks
1 teaspoon vanilla extract
1 cup brandy

In a large microwave-safe bowl, combine milk and sugar. Add cinnamon piece. Microwave on 70% (MEDIUM-HIGH) 12 minutes; do not let mixture boil over. In another large bowl, beat egg yolks and vanilla with an electric mixer until light in color. Remove and discard cinnamon piece from milk mixture. Slowly pour hot milk mixture into egg mixture, beating continually. Cool to room temperature. Stir in brandy. Refrigerate until well chilled. Makes 6 servings.

Clockwise from top: Sangria, page 11; Mexican Hot Chocolate, above; Irish Coffee, page 41.

Tom & Jerry

Hoppel-Poppel *Germany*

This is a hot eggnog holiday favorite found in many countries. The origins are unclear, but it seems to have been around forever.

2 cups eggnog
1/2 cup rum or brandy
Ground nutmeg
4 (2-inch) pieces cinnamon stick

In a 4-cup glass measure, microwave eggnog on 100% (HIGH) 4 to 6 minutes or until hot but not boiling. Stir in rum. Pour into 4 mugs or glasses. Sprinkle each with a pinch of nutmeg and drop in a cinnamon piece. Makes 4 servings.

Spiced Pineapple Punch

Ponche de Pina *Mexico*

This punch does not require fresh pineapple, so it can be made anytime.

1/3 cup sugar
1 cup water
3 (2-inch) pieces cinnamon stick
1 (46-oz.) can pineapple juice
2 cups fresh orange juice
1/2 cup fresh lemon juice

To prepare sugar syrup, in a large microwave-safe bowl, combine sugar and water. Add cinnamon pieces. Microwave on 100% (HIGH) 5 minutes. Let stand 15 minutes. Remove and discard cinnamon pieces, then strain into a serving pitcher. Stir pineapple, orange and lemon juices into sugar syrup. Serve over ice. Makes 2 quarts.

Cooking Tip:
Refrigerate any left over coffee or tea and reheat a single serving in a mug on 100% (HIGH) 1 to 2 minutes.

Wassail

England

This English Christmas drink will really warm you up! Apples are cooked and served in the wassail bowl along with the wassail. It's customary to put a piece of apple into each mug. Variations of this drink differ; some are made similar to an eggnog. I prefer it made only with wine and ale.

4 Red Delicious apples, cored, cut in quarters
1/2 cup sugar
1 cup dry red wine
1/2 teaspoon ground nutmeg
1/8 teaspoon ground cloves
3 (12-oz.) bottles ale or beer
4 (2-inch) pieces cinnamon

Place apples and sugar in a large microwave-safe bowl. Cover tightly. Microwave on 100% (HIGH) 7 to 8 minutes or until apples are tender. Let stand, covered, 5 minutes. Mix in wine, nutmeg, cloves and ale. Add cinnamon pieces. Cover tightly. Microwave on 70% (MEDIUM-HIGH) 12 to 15 minutes or until very hot. Serve a piece of apple in each mug along with wassail. Makes 10 servings.

Coconut Punch

Cremas

Haiti

Fresh coconuts grow wild in Haiti, so you will find them used in everything from drinks to main courses to desserts. This drink resembles an eggnog.

2 cups milk
2 cups flaked sweetened coconut
2 tablespoons sugar
1 to 2 cups light rum
4 eggs, separated
1 teaspoon vanilla extract
1/2 teaspoon finely grated fresh lime peel

To make coconut milk, in a medium-size microwave-safe bowl, combine milk, coconut and sugar. Microwave on 100% (HIGH) 4 minutes or until hot but not boiling. Cool to room temperature. Strain and discard coconut. In a large bowl, beat coconut milk, egg yolks and vanilla. In a medium-size bowl, beat egg whites until stiff, then fold into coconut milk mixture. Refrigerate until ready to serve, up to 24 hours. Sprinkle each serving with lime peel. Makes 4 to 6 servings.

Hot Brandy Alexander

U. S. A.

This makes an elegant after dinner drink. Or serve it by a roaring fire to warm up a wintery evening. If you prefer, substitute rum for the brandy.

1 cup milk
3 teaspoons instant powdered cocoa mix
2/3 cup brandy
2/3 cup whipping cream

In a large bowl, combine milk and cocoa mix. Stir well. Microwave on 100% (HIGH) 1 to 2 minutes or until hot but not boiling. Whisk in brandy and whipping cream until frothy. Pour into 4 small heat-resistant glasses. Makes 4 servings.

Hot Spiced Wine

Glögg *Sweden*

Hearty and warm, this spiced red wine is a wonderful drink after sking or served at a winter party. It has become so popular that many countries claim it as their own.

2 (3-inch) pieces cinnamon stick
4 whole cloves
4 whole cardamom pods
4 cups red Burgundy wine
1/4 cup sugar
1/2 cup golden raisins
1/2 cup bourbon whiskey, if desired
1/4 cup blanched whole almonds

To prepare spice bag, tie up cinnamon, cloves and cardamon pods in an 8-inch-square of cheesecloth. Combine remaining ingredients in a large microwave-safe bowl. Add spice bag. Microwave on 100% (HIGH) 10 to 12 minutes or until very hot but not boiling. Stir until sugar is dissolved. Remove and discard spice bag. Ladle into individual mugs. Makes 6 to 8 servings.

Ground Rice Drink Mix

Horchata de Arroz *Mexico*

This interesting drink is made from boiling rice with cinnamon flavoring. It's a refreshing addition to your next Mexican fiesta.

1 cup water
Powdered sugar, if desired

Rice Puree:
1/2 cup uncooked white rice
3-1/2 cups water
1/4 to 1/2 teaspoon ground cinnamon
1/2 teaspoon cornstarch
3/4 cup powdered sugar

Prepare Rice Puree. In a 2-cup glass measure, combine 2/3 cup of Rice Puree with water. If desired, flavor to taste with powdered sugar. Serve over ice. Makes 2 servings.

Rice Puree:
In a large microwave-safe bowl, combine rice and 2 cups of water. (Be sure bowl is large enough so rice will not boil over.) Cover tightly. Microwave on 100% (HIGH) 8 to 10 minutes or until water comes to a boil. When water boils, microwave on 100% (HIGH) 7 minutes more or until rice is tender. In a blender, process rice, remaining water, cinnamon, cornstarch and powered sugar to a puree. Makes 3-3/4 cups.

Mint Tea

The a la Menthe *Tunisia*

Mint flavored tea is a favorite in countries where the cuisine has been influenced by the Arabs.

4 cups water
2 tablespoons black tea leaves
1-1/2 cups fresh mint leaves
1/3 cup sugar or to taste

In a 4-cup glass measure, microwave water on 100% (HIGH) 10 to 12 minutes or just until it comes to a boil. Place tea and mint leaves in a teapot. Pour in boiling water. Let steep about 10 minutes. Stir in sugar. Makes 6 to 8 servings.

Coffee Grog

England

2 tablespoons light rum
2 tablespoons whipping cream
1 tablespoon dark-brown sugar
Pinch cinnamon-sugar
Pinch ground nutmeg
1 strip lemon peel
1 strip orange peel
2/3 cup hot coffee

Place all ingredients in a microwave-safe coffee cup. Stir to combine flavors. Microwave on 100% (HIGH) 30 seconds or until hot. Makes 1 serving.

After Dinner Coffee

Caffé Espresso *Italy*

Espresso is a very concentrated coffee served with a twist of lemon peel in a demitasse cup. The coffee is ground extra fine to obtain the most flavor.

1 cup espresso
1 twist lemon peel
Sugar, if desired

Prepare espresso with an espresso machine or brew coffee very strong. Pour into a microwave-safe demitasse cup and add a lemon peel twist. Microwave on 100% (HIGH) 30 seconds or until hot. Serve with sugar, if desired. Makes 1 serving.

Coffee with Milk

Cafe Au Lait *France*

1/3 cup milk
1/3 cup strong hot coffee

In a 1-cup glass measure, microwave milk on 100% (HIGH) 45 to 60 seconds or until very hot. Pour steaming milk and coffee into a coffee cup at the same time. Makes 1 serving.

Irish Coffee *(Photo on page 35)*

Ireland

Irish coffee is usually served in a stemmed wine glass rather than a cup. Some say that even though this drink originated in Ireland, it was really a bartender at the Buena Vista in San Francisco, California who made this drink popular.

2 cups water
2 teaspoons instant coffee granules
8 sugar cubes
4 ozs. Irish whiskey
1/4 cup very softly whipped cream

In a 2-cup glass measure, microwave water on 100% (HIGH) 3-1/2 minutes. Stir in coffee granules. Place 2 sugar cubes in each of 4 wine glasses. Slowly pour in hot coffee to within 2 inches of top of each glass. Stir to dissolve sugar. Pour 1 ounce of whiskey into each glass and top with whipped cream. Makes 4 servings.

International Coffees

Coffee is the second largest commodity traded (after oil) in the world. Lore has it that coffee was discovered first in Ethiopia around 900 A.D., but did not become popular in Europe until the 1600's. Americans were by tradition tea drinkers until the Boston Tea Party in 1773.

Coffee is grown in over fifty countries, so it is impossible to attribute any specific recipe for coffee or flavoring to any one country. That is probably why the term "International Coffees" has become so popular. Whether you use the microwave to boil water to make your coffee or to perfectly reheat leftover coffee, you'll enjoy creating any of these coffee combinations with an international flair.

Turkish Coffee

Turk Kahvesi — *Turkey*

Middle Eastern coffee is brewed very strong by American standards. Even when you compare it to Italian espresso or Venezuelan coffee, it's still strong! Luckily it is always served in demitasse cups.

1-1/4 cups water
2 tablespoons sugar
Pinch ground cardamom, if desired
2 tablespoons extra finely ground coffee

Combine all ingredients in a 4-cup glass measure. Microwave on 100% (HIGH) 3 to 4 minutes or until mixture begins to boil. Whisk until well blended. Microwave on 100% (HIGH) 30 to 45 seconds more or until mixture boils and foam rises to top. Spoon foam into 4 demitasse cups. Repeat this boil-spoon process twice, then strain coffee into cups. Makes 4 servings.

Clove-Citrus Flavored Coffee

Café Brûlot — *France*

Cloves give a distinctive flavor to this classic coffee. The word clove comes from the French word clou *meaning nail, which is what whole cloves look like.*

3 tablespoons sugar
Peel 1 orange
Peel 1 lemon
15 whole cloves
3/4 cup brandy
4 cups strong hot coffee

In a large microwave-safe bowl, combine sugar, orange and lemon peels, cloves and brandy. Microwave on 100% (HIGH) 1 to 2 minutes or until mixture begins to steam. Carefully ignite with a match. Let burn until almost all flames are out, then pour in coffee. Ladle flavored coffee into demitasse cups, leaving peels and cloves in bowl. Makes 8 servings.

Soups & Sauces

Soup is one of the most satisfying dishes to create as well as consume. Each culture in the world seems to have created their own type of soup by frugally boiling the ingredients native to their land in liquid. Japan has its simple *miso* soup, a broth with tofu, meat and/or vegetables. Spain calls it *cocido* meaning boiled meat and vegetables. Russian *borsch* and France's *pot au feu* are hearty soups of which you can make an entire meal.

One of the most popular soups in Spain as well as America is a cold tomato based vegetable soup called *gaspacho*. While popular in Spain for many many years, it has only gained American popularity since the 1960's, probably due to the large numbers of Americans traveling abroad.

Mexico has a unique soup known as *sopa seca*—translated it means dry soup. It begins as a liquid soup, but has large quantities of rice or tortillas added that absorb most of the liquid. The final product more closely resembles a stew than a soup. The one dish or pot meal called a casserole in America has its roots in many cultures.

There is no cuisine in the world that has devoted as much effort and time to creating sauces as the French. In fact their classic *Sauce Espagnole* takes three days to prepare. Even the microwave can't help! *Bechamel,* a French innovation of butter, flour and milk, better known as white sauce, is the base for most cream sauces. When chicken, fish or beef stock replaces the milk it is called a *veloute.*

Luckily for cooks, almost any concoction you put on food could be called a sauce. For example in America when you mention sauce you might think of cranberry sauce or hot fudge sauce. In Mexico *salsa* is the popular sauce used for dipping tortilla chips or topping chicken enchiladas. In England a rum cream sauce would top a trifle.

As varied as the types of sauces are, there are only a few techniques you need to know that will help when preparing cooked sauces in the microwave oven.

1. Use a cooking utensil at least twice the volume of your ingredients. Milk and sugar both tend to bubble when they boil. I recommend two- and four-cup glass measures.

2. The cream sauces in this chapter are thickened with flour or cornstarch. You can expect that one cup of sauce will usually thicken in two to three minutes after it comes to a boil. Be sure to cook uncovered.

3. Use a whisk for cream sauces to make sure all ingredients are blended smooth. Stirring all sauces is important to blend ingredients and for even cooking.

Meatball Soup

Sopa Albondigas — *Mexico*

Meatball soup is served by almost every Mexican restaurant and each has their own recipe. This recipe is my favorite, a combination of many I have tasted.

3/4 lb. ground beef
1/4 lb. chorizo sausage
1 tablespoon chopped fresh parsley
1 egg, beaten
1/2 cup dry bread crumbs
1 medium-size onion, chopped
1 tablespoon vegetable oil
6 cups beef broth

In a large bowl, combine beef, chorizo, parsley, egg and bread crumbs. Mix well. Shape in 1-inch balls. Place meat balls in a single layer in a flat microwave-safe casserole dish. Cover loosley. Microwave on 100% (HIGH) 4 minutes. Turn balls over, re-cover and microwave on 100% (HIGH) 2 to 4 minutes more or until meatballs are no longer pink in center. In a large microwave-safe bowl, place onion and vegetable oil. Microwave on 100% (HIGH) 3 minutes or until onions are tender. Pour in beef broth and add meat balls. Microwave on 100% (HIGH) 12 to 15 minutes or until broth begins to boil. Makes 4 servings.

Vegetable Soup

Minestrone — *Italy*

Minestrone *is a hearty vegetable soup often served as a meal in itself. In Italian* minestra *means soup and* minestrone *means a big soup. Serve this with warm crispy Italian bread.*

1/2 medium-size onion, finely chopped
1/2 cup thinly sliced unpeeled zucchini
1/2 cup sliced celery
1/2 cup thinly sliced carrots
2 tablespoons olive oil
1 (16-oz.) can tomatoes, chopped, juice reserved
1 (16-oz.) can white beans (Cannellini)
4 cups beef broth
1 teaspoon crushed dried basil
1 teaspoon crushed dried oregano
Salt and black pepper to taste
1/2 cup freshly grated Parmesan cheese

In a large microwave-safe bowl, combine onion, zucchini, celery, carrots and olive oil. Cover tightly. Microwave on 100% (HIGH) 4 to 5 minutes or until all vegetables are tender. Add tomatoes with reserved juice, beans with juice, beef broth, basil and oregano. Microwave on 100% (HIGH) 12 to 15 minutes or until soup comes to a boil. Season with salt and pepper. Serve with Parmesan cheese to sprinkle over individual servings. Makes 4 to 6 servings.

Senegalese Soup

Épicé Soupe — *Africa*

Although curry is not generally associated with African food, it is thought that the French transported some curry-flavored dishes from India to West Africa in their colonizing days. When you taste this cold soup, you'll understand how refreshing it would be on a hot African day.

2 (4-oz.) chicken breast halves
1 medium-size onion, finely chopped
1 medium-size cooking apple, peeled, cored, diced
1/2 cup diced celery
1 to 2 teaspoons curry powder
2 tablespoons butter or margarine
2 tablespoons all-purpose flour
6 cups chicken broth
1 cup whipping cream
Salt and black pepper to taste

Wrap each chicken breast half in plastic wrap. Microwave on 100% (HIGH) 4 to 5 minutes or until no longer pink in center. Set aside to cool. In a large microwave-safe bowl, combine onion, apple, celery, curry powder and butter. Cover tightly. Microwave on 100% (HIGH) 2 to 3 minutes or until celery is tender. Stir in flour. Microwave on 100% (HIGH) 30 seconds. Add 2 cups chicken broth. In a food processor fitted with the metal blade or a blender, process chicken broth mixture to a puree. In a large bowl, combine puree, remaining 4 cups of chicken broth and cream. Season with salt and pepper. Mix well. Dice cooked chicken and stir into soup. Refrigerate overnight or until well chilled. Makes 4 to 6 servings.

Fruit Soup

Fruktsuppe — *Sweden*

My great-grandfather was Swedish and as a child I could never appreciate this type of soup. Because dried fruits are used, it can be made any time.

1 cup dried apricots
1 cup dried apples
1/2 cup pitted prunes
4 cups apple juice
1 small piece cinnamon stick
1 teaspoon freshly grated lemon peel
1 teaspoon freshly grated orange peel

In a large microwave-safe bowl, combine all ingredients. Cover tightly. Microwave on 100% (HIGH) 10 minutes. Stir. Re-cover and microwave on 100% (HIGH) 5 minutes more. Let stand covered until soup reaches room temperature. Refrigerate overnight to blend flavors. Remove and discard cinnamon piece before serving. Makes 4 to 6 servings.

Squash Soup

U. S. A.

Squash is a native American vegetable, one of the few we have. It is a very adaptable vegetable, and can be baked, boiled, sauteed and best of all, it cooks perfectly in the microwave.

1 lb. squash (banana, butternut, summer or zucchini)
4 slices bacon
1/2 medium-size onion
1 (16-oz.) can tomatoes, chopped, juice reserved
3 cups beef bouillon
2 tablespoons chopped fresh parsley
1/2 teaspoon dried oregano
1/4 teaspoon dried thyme
1/4 cup dry sherry

If needed, peel squash and remove seeds. Cut in 1-inch cubes. Place in a large microwave-safe bowl. Cover tightly. Microwave on 100% (HIGH) 4 to 7 minutes or until tender. Let stand covered until ready to use. Place bacon in a microwave-safe dish and cover with a paper towel. Microwave on 100% (HIGH) 4 to 5 minutes or until crisp. Remove bacon, drain on paper towels and crumble. Microwave onion in remaining fat on 100% (HIGH) 2 to 3 minutes or until tender. Drain off fat. In a large microwave-safe serving bowl, combine squash, bacon, onion, tomatoes with reserved juice, beef bouillon, parsley, oregano and thyme. Cover tightly. Microwave on 100% (HIGH) 10 to 12 minutes or until mixture boils. Stir sherry into soup just before serving. Makes 4 servings.

Crab & Mushroom Soup

Moo Goo Tang — *China*

If good fresh or frozen crab is not available, I suggest you try the imitation crab now widely available. It is really quite good and the price is much more reasonable. Oriental sesame oil has a very distinct flavor which is similar to its aroma. Add it only if you like it.

3 green onions, cut in 1-inch pieces
1 medium-size carrot, cut in 1-inch julienne strips
1/2 cup thinly sliced fresh mushrooms
4 cups chicken broth
8 ozs. crab meat
1/2 cup chopped fresh cilantro leaves
3 or 4 drops oriental sesame oil, if desired

In a large microwave-safe bowl, combine green onions, carrot and mushrooms. Cover tightly. Microwave on 100% (HIGH) 1-1/2 to 2 minutes or until carrot is tender. Add chicken broth. Microwave on 100% (HIGH) 10 to 12 minutes or until mixture comes to a boil. Stir in crab, cilantro and sesame oil, if desired. Microwave on 100% (HIGH) 2 to 3 minutes more or until heated to serving temperature. Makes 4 servings.

Vichyssoise (Leek & Potato Soup)

U. S. A.

This classic American soup has a French name because it was invented by a French chef named Louis Diat. Working in New York in 1925, he named the soup after his home town, Vichy.

3 leeks, cleaned, white part only, chopped
1/2 medium-size onion, chopped
3 medium-size boiling potatoes, peeled, diced
3 cups chicken broth
1/2 teaspoon salt, if desired
2 cups milk or half and half or 1 cup milk and 1 cup half and half
1 tablespoon snipped fresh chives

In a large microwave-safe casserole dish, combine leeks, onion and potatoes. Cover tightly. Microwave on 100% (HIGH) 8 to 10 minutes or until potatoes are tender. Uncover and let stand 10 minutes. In a food processor fitted with the metal blade or a blender, process potato mixture and chicken broth to a puree. If necessary, process in 2 or 3 batches. Stir in salt, if desired, and milk. Refrigerate until well chilled. Garnish soup with chives. Makes 4 servings.

Beet Soup

Borsch — *Russia*

Borsch—even the spelling is questionable! That lovely beet colored vegetable soup has only two certainties regarding ingredients, beets and sour cream!

1 medium-size onion, finely chopped
1 medium-size carrot, finely chopped
3/4 lb. beets, peeled, diced or 1 (16-oz.) can beets, diced
2 cups shredded cabbage
4 cups beef broth or tomato juice
Salt and black pepper to taste
Dairy sour cream

In a large microwave-safe bowl, combine onion, carrots and beets. Cover tightly. Microwave on 100% (HIGH) 3 to 4 minutes or until vegetables are until tender. Add cabbage, re-cover and microwave on 100% (HIGH) 3 minutes. Stir in beef broth. Season with salt and pepper. Re-cover and microwave on 100% (HIGH) 12 to 15 minutes. Refrigerate overnight or until well chilled. Top each serving with a large dollop of sour cream. Makes 4 servings.

Potato Leek Soup in Bread Bowls

Potage en Croute — *France*

Soup served in a bread "bowl" is as attractive as it is tasty. It blends a country French feeling to any meal. If you prefer to use a different soup, I recommend you stay with a creamy type.

3 medium-size boiling potatoes, peeled, diced
3 leeks, cleaned, thinly sliced
3 cups chicken broth
1/4 teaspoon salt
1/4 teaspoon black pepper
Pinch ground nutmeg
4 (6-inch) round French bread loaves
1/4 cup olive oil
1 garlic clove, minced
1-1/2 cups whipping cream
Fresh dill sprig and additional leek slices to garnish

In a large microwave-safe bowl, combine potatoes and leeks. Cover tightly. Microwave on 100% (HIGH) 8 to 10 minutes or until soft. Let stand 5 minutes and uncover. In a food processor fitted with the metal blade or a blender, process potatoes and leeks to a puree. If using a blender, add a small amount of chicken broth. Wash microwave-safe bowl; return puree to bowl. Combine puree, chicken broth, salt, pepper and nutmeg. Cover tightly. Microwave on 100% (HIGH) 12 to 15 minutes or until mixture comes to a boil. Meanwhile, preheat oven to 350F (175C). Using a sharp knife, slice off top of each bread round. Cut around each leaving a 3/4-inch edge. Scoop out bread; reserve for another use. In a 1-cup measure, combine olive oil and garlic. Brush inside of each loaf. Place on a baking sheet. Bake in preheated oven about 10 minutes or until toasted. If needed, reheat soup on 70% (MEDIUM HIGH) until hot. Stir cream into hot soup. Ladle into toasted loaves. Garnish with dill sprig and additional sliced leek. Serve at once. The bread can and should be eaten after the soup is finished. Makes 4 servings.

Potato Leek Soup in Bread Bowls, above.

Onion Soup

Soupe à l'Oignon — *France*

Nothing tastes better on a cool day than a tureen of flavorful onion soup topped with bubbling hot cheese. The better the beef bouillon, the richer tasting the soup. This soup tastes even better made a day ahead.

1/4 cup butter or margarine
4 cups thinly sliced Spanish onions
4 (10-1/2-oz.) cans condensed beef bouillon
4 slices French bread, toasted
1/2 cup grated Gruyère cheese
2 tablespoons freshly grated Parmesan cheese
1/4 cup dry sherry

In a large microwave-safe bowl, place butter and onions. Microwave on 100% (HIGH) 8 to 10 minutes or until onions are well done but not brown, stirring twice during cooking. Add beef bouillon. Microwave on 70% (MEDIUM HIGH) 15 minutes. Meanwhile, preheat broiler. Place toasted French bread on a baking sheet. Sprinkle each piece of bread with Gruyère and Parmesan cheese. Broil just until cheese bubbles, about 1 minute. Stir sherry into soup. Ladle into serving bowls. Top each bowl of soup with a slice of cheese-topped bread. Makes 4 servings.

Tortilla Soup

Sopa de Tortillas — *Mexico*

Crisp tortilla chips are placed in individual serving bowls, then topped with a cheese and vegetable soup.

1/4 cup onion, finely chopped
1/4 cup diced celery
2 tablespoons diced green bell pepper
1/4 cup diced tomato
3 cups chicken stock
1 teaspoon dried leaf oregano
1/4 teaspoon garlic powder
1/4 teaspoon black pepper
Salt to taste
2 cups tortilla chips
3/4 cup shredded Cheddar cheese
3/4 cup shredded Monterey Jack cheese

In a large microwave-safe bowl, combine onion, celery, bell pepper and tomato. Cover tightly. Microwave on 100% (HIGH) 3 to 4 minutes or until vegetables are soft. Add chicken stock, oregano, garlic and black pepper. Season with salt. Re-cover and microwave on 100% (HIGH) 8 to 10 minutes or until soup starts to boil. To serve, divide tortilla chips among 4 soup bowls. Sprinkle with cheeses and ladle soup into bowls. Makes 4 to 6 servings.

Hot & Sour Soup

Suan La Tang — *China*

Pungent and tasty at the same time is a good description of this spicy, yet sour soup.

5 cups chicken broth

1/2 lb. fresh mushrooms, thinly sliced

1/2 lb. lean pork, cut in thin strips

1/4 cup plus 1 tablespoon white vinegar

3 tablespoons soy sauce

1/2 teaspoon red pepper flakes, crushed

1/4 teaspoon black pepper

1/4 lb. tofu, drained, diced

3 tablespoons cornstarch

1/2 cup cold water

1 egg, beaten

2 teaspoons sesame oil

1/2 cup sliced green onions

Pour chicken broth into a large microwave-safe bowl. Microwave on 100% (HIGH) 12 to 15 minutes or until broth starts to boil. Stir in mushrooms, pork, vinegar, soy sauce, red pepper flakes and black pepper. Microwave on 100% (HIGH) 5 minutes. Add tofu. In a 1-cup measure, dissolve cornstarch in cold water, then stir into hot soup. Microwave on 100% (HIGH) 3 to 4 minutes. Slowly pour in beaten egg while stirring soup. Sprinkle soup with sesame oil and green onion. Makes 6 to 8 servings.

Buttermilk Chowder

U. S. A.

Pure Americana. This soup combines the classic chowder ingredients—corn, potatoes and bacon. Serve it with a hearty cornbread for a North East supper.

3 slices bacon, diced

1/4 cup diced onion

2 medium-size boiling potatoes, peeled, diced

2 tablespoons all-purpose flour

2 cups fresh corn or 1 (10-oz.) pkg. frozen corn

2 cups chicken broth

2 cups buttermilk

In a large microwave-safe bowl, combine bacon, onion and potatoes. Cover tightly. Microwave on 100% (HIGH) 4 minutes. Stir. Re-cover and microwave on 100% (HIGH) 2 to 4 minutes more or until potatoes are tender. Sprinkle flour over potato mixture and stir to mix. Stir in corn and chicken broth. Microwave on 100 % (HIGH) 10 to 12 minutes or until mixture starts to thicken. Stir in buttermilk. Microwave on 100% (HIGH) 2 to 3 minutes more just to heat; do not boil. Makes 4 to 6 servings.

Canadian Cheddar Soup

Canada

Canada is well known for its robust Cheddar cheese.

1 cup diced carrots
1/4 cup diced celery
1 cup diced onion
1/2 cup diced parsnip
2 tablespoons butter or margarine
1/4 cup all-purpose flour
4 cups beef broth
3/4 lb. sharp Cheddar cheese, shredded (3 cups)
2 cups milk

In a large deep microwave-safe casserole dish, combine carrots, celery, onion, parsnips and butter. Cover tightly. Microwave on 100% (HIGH) 8 minutes. Stir in flour until completely mixed. Pour in beef broth. Re-cover and microwave on 100% (HIGH) 10 minutes or until mixture comes to a boil, stirring after 5 minutes. Stir in cheese until smooth, then stir in milk. Microwave on 100% (HIGH) 2 to 3 minutes or until serving temperature, being careful not to boil soup or overcook cheese. Makes 6 servings.

Good Woman Soup (Vegetable Soup)

Potage Bonne Femme

France

What a wonderful name! Knowing the English translation makes a dish more interesting.

2 leeks, cleaned, white part only, thinly sliced
3 medium-size carrots, thinly sliced
2 medium-size boiling potatoes, peeled, diced
1 stalk celery, thinly sliced
1/4 cup butter or margarine
3 cups chicken stock
Salt and black pepper to taste
1/2 cup whipping cream

In a large microwave-safe cassrole dish, combine leeks, carrots, potatoes and celery. Dot vegetables with butter. Cover tightly. Microwave on 100% (HIGH) 8 to 10 minutes or until vegetables are tender. Let stand, covered, 5 minutes. In a food processor fitted with the metal blade or a blender, process vegetables and chicken stock to a puree. If necessary, process in 2 batches. Wash casserole dish. Pour puree into casserole dish. Cover tightly. Microwave on 100% (HIGH) 8 to 10 minutes or until mixture simmers. Season with salt and pepper. Stir in cream. Makes 4 servings.

Curried Consomme

I n d i a

Mention curry and everyone thinks of India. This quick soup has an exotic combination of flavors.

1-1/4 cups chicken broth
1 cup half and half
1/2-1 teaspoon curry powder
Pinch of ground ginger
1/2 cup finely chopped apple
2 tablespoons toasted flaked coconut

In a medium-size microwave-safe bowl, combine chicken broth, half and half, curry powder and ginger. Microwave on 100% (HIGH) 3 minutes. Stir in apple and coconut. Microwave on 100% (HIGH) 2 to 3 minutes more or until hot. Makes 4 servings.

Chicken Broth with Julienne Cut Vegetables

Consomme Julienne

F r a n c e

Clear broth with jewel colored vegetables, this consomme is beautiful and tasty enough to serve at any meal.

2 cups chicken broth
1 medium-size carrot, cut in julienne strips
1 green onion, cut in julienne strips
1 small turnip, cut in julienne strips

Pour chicken broth into a large microwave-safe bowl. Microwave on 100% (HIGH) 6 minutes or until broth comes to a boil. Add carrot, green onion and turnip. Microwave on 100% (HIGH) 2 to 3 minutes more or until vegetables are tender. Makes 4 servings.

Italian Tomato Sauce

Salsa Marinara — *Italy*

This zesty tomato sauce can be used to top pasta, seafood, poultry or even stirred into a hearty vegetable soup. Make a double batch and freeze one.

2 lbs. plum tomatoes (about 16), seeded, coarsely chopped
2 shallots, coarsely chopped
1 stalk celery, chopped
2 tablespoons olive oil
1 teaspoon red wine vinegar
1/4 teaspoon dried leaf thyme
1/4 teaspoon dried leaf basil
1/4 teaspoon dried leaf oregano
1/2 teaspoon dried leaf rosemary
1 teaspoon sugar
1 bay leaf

In a food processor fitted with the metal blade or a blender, process tomatoes, shallots, celery, olive oil, vinegar, thyme, basil, oregano, rosemary and sugar with on/off turns until just combined. Do not overmix. Pour into a medium-size microwave-safe bowl. Bury bay leaf in sauce. Microwave on 100% (HIGH) 6 minutes or until thickened, stirring several times during cooking. Let stand 10 minutes. Remove and discard bay leaf. Stir before serving. Makes about 2 cups.

Basic Curry Sauce

Susu Curry Sauce — *India*

Serve this curry sauce over any combination of vegetables, beef, lamb, seafood or chicken. Increase or decrease the amount of curry powder to suit your own tastes. Remember, most curry powder has cayenne pepper, so the more you add, the hotter it will be.

1 medium-size onion, diced
1 medium-size cooking apple, peeled and diced
1 stalk celery, diced
2 tablespoons butter or margarine
1 tablespoon curry powder
2 tablespoons cornstarch
1 cup chicken stock
3 cups milk
Salt to taste

Place onion, apple, celery, butter and curry powder in a large microwave-safe casserole dish. Cover tightly. Microwave on 100% (HIGH) 3 to 5 minutes or until all are tender. In a 2-cup measure, dissolve cornstarch in chicken stock. Pour into onion mixture, then add milk. Stir well. Microwave on 100% (HIGH) 10 to 12 minutes or until mixture simmers and thickens slightly. Makes about 5 cups.

Basic White Sauce

Sauce Béchamel — *France*

A most versatile sauce, this can be used by itself as a topping for vegetables or with cheese added as the basis for macaroni and cheese. It is also the base used for savory soufflés.

2 tablespoons butter or margarine
2 tablespoons all-purpose flour
1 cup milk
1/8 teaspoon salt

In a small microwave-safe bowl, microwave butter on 100% (HIGH) 30 to 60 seconds or until melted. Stir in flour. Microwave on 100% (HIGH) 30 seconds. Stir in milk and salt. Microwave on 100% (HIGH) 4 to 5 minutes or until mixture comes to a boil and begins to thicken. Makes 1-1/4 cups.

Variations:
To prepare *Sauce Velouté,* substitute 1 cup chicken, beef or fish stock for milk.
To prepare *Mornay Sauce,* stir in 1 tablespoon freshly grated Parmesan cheese and 2 tablespoons grated Gruyère cheese after sauce has thickened.

Light Custard Sauce

Crème Anglaise — *France*

This is really considered a very bland boiled custard, hence the name English Cream. It is rarely eaten as a custard, but instead as a sauce.

2 cups milk or half and half
1/4 cup sugar
3 eggs, beaten
1 teaspoon vanilla extract

In a medium-size microwave-safe bowl, combine milk and sugar. Microwave on 100% (HIGH) 5 to 5-1/2 minutes or until mixture is very hot but not boiling. In a small bowl, slowly stir about 1/2 cup of hot mixture into beaten eggs. Whisk egg mixture back into hot mixture. Microwave on 50% (MEDIUM) 2 minutes, stirring twice during cooking. Microwave on 30% (LOW) 4 to 5 minutes or until thickened, stirring twice during cooking. Stir in vanilla. If custard curdles, strain through a fine strainer or process in a food processor fitted with the metal blade to a puree. Serve warm or chilled. Makes 2 cups.

Quick Béarnaise Sauce

Sauce Béarnaise

France

This easy version has the taste of the classic sauce. It was named after Henry IV, a native of the province of Bearn in southern France.

1 (3-oz.) pkg. cream cheese
2 eggs yolks, beaten
1 teaspoon minced onion
2 tablespoons dry white wine
1 teaspoon dried leaf tarragon
1/2 teaspoon dried leaf chervil

In a 2-cup glass measure, microwave cream cheese on 100% (HIGH) 20 seconds or until softened. Stir in egg yolks, onion, wine, tarragon and chervil. Microwave on 100% (HIGH) 45 seconds or until warm, stirring every 15 seconds. Makes 2/3 cup.

Cumberland Sauce (Photo on page 121)

England

This is a bright red sauce made with currant jelly that goes well with beef, ham or wild game. It originated in England and probably came over with early American settlers.

1 cup red currant jelly
1/4 teaspoon dry mustard
1/8 teaspoon ground cloves
1/8 teaspoon ground ginger
1/4 cup port wine
1/4 cup fresh orange juice
1/4 cup dark raisins

In a small microwave-safe bowl, microwave jelly on 100% (HIGH) 1 minute. Stir to soften. Mix in dry mustard, cloves, ginger, wine, orange juice and raisins. Microwave on 100% (HIGH) 1 to 1-1/2 minutes or until thickened. Stir until smooth. Serve warm or cold. Makes 1-1/2 cups.

Peanut Dipping Sauce *(Photo on page 67)*

Indonesia

Indonesia, Malaysia and Thailand all lay claim to this peanut flavored sauce. It is usually served as a condiment with skewered lamb, beef, chicken or shrimp.

1/3 cup smooth peanut butter
1/3 cup coconut or regular milk
2 tablespoons finely chopped onion
1 clove garlic, very finely chopped
1 tablespoon soy sauce
1 tablespooon fresh lemon or lime juice
1/4 teaspoon crushed dried red pepper flakes

Combine all ingredients in a small microwave-safe bowl. Microwave on 100% (HIGH) 1 minute. Stir until smooth. Makes 1 cup.

Plum Sauce

Ume Shu

Japan

This is an Americanized version of the tasty plum sauce served as a dipping sauce or with such Japanese favorites as shredded pork. The original sauce calls for dried plums, which are not easy to obtain.

1/2 cup plum preserves
1 teaspoon instant chicken bouillon granules
2 tablespoons rice vinegar
1-1/2 teaspoons soy sauce
1/2 teaspoon Chinese five-spice powder

Combine all ingredients in a small microwave-safe bowl. Microwave on 100% (HIGH) 3 minutes. Stir. Microwave on 100% (HIGH) 1 to 2 minutes more or until well heated. Makes 1/2 cup.

Nut-Flavored Butter

Burre Noisetts *France*

Serve this butter over cooked vegetables or fish for a delightful new taste.

1/2 cup butter

In a flat-bottom microwave-safe dish, microwave butter on 100% (HIGH) until melted, then continue microwaving 2 to 5 minutes or just until butter begins to turn brown. Use quickly. Makes 1/2 cup.

Cranberry Chutney

U. S. A.

Chutney originated in India where it is spelled chatni. *It is a savory-sweet combination of local fruits and spices. The cranberry is considered an American original, so I have combined it with sugars and spices to make this chutney.*

1 medium-size onion, chopped
1 medium-size cooking apple, peeled, cored, chopped
1/4 cup chopped celery
1 (12-oz.) pkg. fresh or frozen cranberries, thawed if frozen
3/4 cup granulated sugar
1/4 cup light-brown sugar
1/2 cup dark raisins
1 teaspoon ground cinnamon
3/4 teaspoon ground ginger
1/2 teaspoon ground allspice
1/2 cup water

In a large microwave safe bowl, combine onion, apple and celery. Cover tightly. Microwave on 100% (HIGH) 4 minutes or until all are tender. Stir in cranberries, sugars, raisins, cinnamon, ginger, allspice and water. Re-cover and microwave on 100% (HIGH) 8 to 10 minutes or until cranberries start to pop. Stir. Re-cover and let stand 15 minutes. Makes about 3 cups.

Pineapple & Horseradish Baste

U. S. A.

Brush this baste over chicken, shrimp, ham or pork before and during cooking.

1 cup apricot-pineapple preserves
1/4 cup grated fresh or prepared horseradish
1/4 cup prepared mustard

Combine all ingredients in a small microwave-safe bowl. Blend well. Microwave on 100% (HIGH) 3 minutes. Makes about 1-1/2 cups.

Horseradish Jelly

U. S. A.

I first tasted this in a small housewares' store in Connecticut and thought it was a great takeoff on the traditional jalapeño jelly.

1-1/4 cups white wine vinegar
1/3 cup prepared horseradish
3/4 cup water
3 cups sugar
1 (3-oz.) pouch liquid pectin

In a 2-cup glass measure, microwave vinegar on 100% (HIGH) 4 minutes or until vinegar comes to a boil. Stir in horseradish. Cover tightly. Let stand overnight. Sterilize 3 (1/2-pint) jars and covers. Keep hot until needed. Strain vinegar mixture through a fine sieve or cheese cloth. Vinegar should measure 1 cup. If necessary, add additional vinegar. In a medium-size microwave-safe bowl, combine vinegar, water and sugar. Microwave on 100% (HIGH) 5 to 6 minutes or until mixture comes to a full boil. Stir in pectin. Microwave on 100% (HIGH) 3 minutes or until mixture comes back to a boil. Boil 1 minute. Skim off foam. Ladle jelly into hot jars. Wipe rim of jar with a clean damp cloth. Cool and spoon a 1/4-inch layer of melted paraffin over jelly, covering completely. Attach covers. Makes 3 (1/2-pint) jars.

Caramel Sauce

U. S. A.

This buttery caramel sauce is great on ice cream, swirled into tapioca pudding or served as a rich sauce for bread pudding.

1 cup light-brown sugar
3/4 cup whipping cream
2 tablespoons butter or margarine
1 teaspoon vanilla extract

In a small microwave-safe bowl, combine brown sugar, whipping cream and butter. Microwave on 100% (HIGH) 3 to 5 minutes or until mixture comes to a boil. Stir in vanilla. Makes 1-1/2 cups.

Chocolate Fudge Sauce

U. S. A.

I developed this sauce when trying to make my favorite fudge sauce. Out of whipping cream, I substituted sour cream and everyone loved my creation! My favorite way to serve this is lukewarm with a plate of cut up fresh fruit to dip in fondue-style.

1/2 cup unsweetened cocoa powder
1 cup sugar
1 cup dairy sour cream
1 teaspoon vanilla extract

In a small microwave-safe bowl, combine cocoa powder and sugar. Mix in sour cream. Microwave on 100% (HIGH) 1 minute. Stir. Microwave on 100% (HIGH) 2 minutes more, stirring twice during cooking to completely combine ingredients. Stir in vanilla. Makes 1-1/2 cups.

Salads

In America our green salad is almost an institution. Lettuce and tomatoes tossed with a dressing is served in almost every restaurant across the country, regardless of the type of food they serve. Growing up on the West Coast, I took for granted the year-round availability of fresh, beautiful vegetables. Shopping for lettuce in the Midwest in midwinter years ago was a real eye opener. The ingredients used in salad making are determined by what is available, not only in countries around the world, but in America as well.

In Spain salads are served as a first course, as it usually is here in America. The ingredients are similar too, lettuce and tomatoes with creative additions of an assortment of vegetables. The one difference is that Spanish salads usually have the ingredients neatly arranged on the plate instead of all tossed together in a bowl.

Italians often prepare an assortment of vegetables and meat combinations marinated in olive oil, vinegar and herbs. These salads are usually set out buffet style for their antipasto and served chilled or at room temperature.

Chinese salads generally consist of crisp chilled vegetables tossed with a light sesame or vegetable oil. They often add a pinch of sugar to bring out delicate flavors. You will find that often meat or seafood has been combined with the vegetables to expand the salad into an entire meal. Chinese chicken salad is a perfect Americanized example. Chicken pieces are tossed with lettuce and crisp fried noodles and topped with a soy-garlic sesame dressing.

Garlic seems to be the universal spice found in everything from salads to soups in almost all cultures from Chinese to Spanish to French. The technique of rubbing a salad bowl with a piece of garlic is thought to have originated in France to add just a hint of this overpowering flavor.

A *salade verte* (green salad) is served daily in French homes at the midday meal or with supper. But they prefer to serve it after the main course, instead of before, so that it is a kind of light bridge preceeding dessert. Vinaigrette with a hint of mustard and herbs is the preferred dressing since it enhances the natural flavors of the ingredients. Their one precaution is to go lightly on the vinegar so it's flavor doesn't interfere with the wine being served!

Warm Potato Salad with Bacon

Warmer Kartoffelsalat mit Speck — *Germany*

Potatoes are a mainstay in the German diet, so much so that you might be served two types of potatoes in one meal.

6 medium-size boiling potatoes, peeled, cut in 1/2-inch cubes
4 slices bacon
1/2 medium-size onion, chopped
1/2 teaspoon salt
1 tablespoon all-purpose flour
1/3 cup cider vinegar
1/4 cup sugar
1/2 cup water

Place potatoes in a microwave-safe bowl. Cover tightly. Microwave on 100% (HIGH) 10 minutes. Gently stir to rearrange. Re-cover and microwave on 100% (HIGH) 4 to 5 minutes more. Let stand, covered, 10 minutes. Place bacon in a flat microwave-safe casserole dish. Cover with a paper towel. Microwave on 100% (HIGH) 5 minutes or until crisp. Drain on a paper towel. To prepare dressing, stir onion into bacon fat. Microwave on 100% (HIGH) 2 minutes or until onion is tender. Stir in salt and flour. Microwave on 100% (HIGH) 30 seconds. Mix in vinegar, sugar and water. Microwave on 100% (HIGH) 1 to 2 minutes or until boiling, stirring once during cooking. Crumble bacon. Add bacon and dressing to potatoes. Toss gently. Spoon into a serving bowl. Serve warm. Makes 6 servings.

Potato Salad

Salade Pommes — *France*

Potato salad with a vinegrette dressing is a nice light accommpaniment to any meal. Add leftover vegetables for a different flavor and more color.

4 medium-size boiling potatoes, peeled, diced
1/4 cup thinly sliced green onions
1 tablespoon chopped fresh basil
1/2 cup vinegrette dressing

Place potatoes in a microwave-safe bowl. Cover tightly. Microwave on 100% (HIGH) 6 to 8 minutes or until tender. Let stand 5 minutes before uncovering. Stir in green onions, basil and vinegrette dressing. Spoon into a serving bowl. Serve warm or refrigerate until chilled. Makes 4 servings.

Tangy Chicken Potato Salad

U. S. A.

Most people don't consider salad dressing a marinade, but it really is, especially when the salad is refrigerated overnight to blend the flavors.

4 (4-oz.) chicken breasts, deboned
4 medium-size new potatoes
1/3 cup olive oil
1/3 cup red wine vinegar
1 large shallot, minced
1 tablespoon snipped fresh parsley
1/2 teaspoon crushed dried leaf rosemary
1/2 teaspoon seasoned salt
1/4 teaspoon black pepper
4 green onions, sliced
1/2 medium-size red bell pepper, cut in 1/4-inch cubes

Wrap each chicken breast tightly in plastic wrap. Place in microwave oven on a paper towel. Microwave on 100% (HIGH) 3 to 5 minutes or until fully cooked. Let stand 5 minutes before unwrapping. Pierce potatoes 3 or 4 times with a fork. Microwave on 100% (HIGH) 5 minutes. Turn potatoes over. Microwave on 100% (HIGH) 4 to 5 minutes more or until tender. To make dressing, in a salad bowl, whisk olive oil, vinegar, shallot, parsley, rosemary, seasoned salt and black pepper. Cut chicken in 1/4-inch-wide strips. Peel potatoes, if desired, and cut in 1/4-inch slices. Add chicken, potatoes, green onions and bell pepper to dressing. Toss to mix well. For best flavor, cover and refrigerate overnight. Serve warm or cold. Makes 4 to 6 servings.

Marinated Vegetable Salad

U. S. A.

The vegetables are raw, and the salad dressing is cooked and used for a marinade. This is a great make-ahead recipe.

1 medium-size unpeeled cucumber, thinly sliced
1 medium-size unpeeled yellow or green zucchini, thinly sliced
1/2 medium-size red bell pepper, thinly sliced
1 cup shredded green cabbage
1/4 cup cider vinegar
3 tablespoons honey
1/4 cup vegetable oil
1/2 teaspoon salt
1/4 teaspoon poppy seeds

In a large bowl, combine cucumber, zucchini, bell pepper and cabbage. In a 1-cup glass measure, combine vinegar, honey, oil, salt and poppy seeds. Microwave on 100% (HIGH) 2 minutes or until mixture begins to boil. Stir well and pour over vegetables. Toss to mix well. Cover and refrigerate at least 6 hours before serving. Makes 4 to 6 servings.

Two Bean Salad

Salade Haricort Verte *France*

Marinated bean bundles with pimiento ties make this a pretty, tasty and elegant salad.

1/3 lb. fresh green beans
1/3 lb. fresh wax beans
1/2 cup rice vinegar
1/2 cup olive oil
1 tablespoon Dijon-style mustard
1/2 teaspoon minced fresh dill
1 (2-oz.) jar whole pimiento

Trim only stem end of beans. Place in a flat microwave-safe dish. Cover tightly. Microwave on 100% (HIGH) 2 to 3 minutes or just until beans are tender. In a small bowl, whisk vinegar, olive oil, mustard and dill. Pour over beans. Refrigerate 1 hour to chill or serve warm. To serve, divide beans in 4 equal bundles. Cut pimiento in 8 long strips. Set bundles of beans on a serving platter and wrap pimiento around center of each forming an "X". Makes 4 servings.

Carrot Salad

Shelada Ghezo *Morroco*

This salad is great to serve with a beef roast or ham. It tastes best when served well chilled.

3/4 lb. carrots, peeled, sliced
1/2 cup raisins
1/4 cup chopped fresh parsley
1 tablespoon fresh lemon juice
1 teaspoon sugar
2 tablespoons vegetable oil
1/8 teaspoon ground cinnamon
1/8 teaspoon ground cumin

Place carrots in a large microwave-safe bowl. Cover tightly. Microwave on 100% (HIGH) 3 to 4 minutes or until tender. Stir in raisins. Let stand, covered, 5 minutes. Rinse under cold running water to cool quickly. In a serving bowl, combine carrots, raisins, parsley, lemon juice, sugar, vegetable oil, cinnamon and cumin. Refrigerate until ready to serve. Makes 4 servings.

Bell Pepper Salad

Insalata di Peperonata — *Italy*

The skin of bell peppers has always been difficult but necessary to remove for best taste appeal. Wrapping the peppers individually and steaming them in the microwave oven works great. It makes the skin easy to peel.

4 red, green or yellow bell peppers or a combination
1/4 cup olive oil
1 tablespoon capers
1 garlic clove, minced
1 teaspoon dried leaf rosemary, crushed
2 tablespoons white wine vinegar

Remove core and seeds from bell peppers. Wrap each bell pepper tightly in plastic wrap. Microwave on 100% (HIGH) 10 minutes. If bell peppers are still firm at all, microwave on 100% (HIGH) 1 to 2 minutes more. Remove any that are completely soft. Let stand until room temperature before unwrapping. Using a sharp paring knife, remove skin. Cut peeled bell peppers in 1/2-inch wide-strips. In a 1-cup glass measure, combine olive oil, capers, garlic and rosemary. Microwave on 100% (HIGH) 1 minute to heat oil and bring out flavors. Mix in vinegar and pour over bell peppers. Serve at room temperature. Makes 4 servings.

Tossed Onion Salad

Insalata di Cipolle — *Italy*

Once cooked onions loose their pungent flavor and are tossed with olive oil, herbs and Parmesan cheese, they take on a wonderful mellow flavor.

3 bunches green onions, cut in 3-inch pieces
1 large red onion, thinly sliced, separated in rings
1 bay leaf
1/4 cup olive oil
2 tablespoons white wine vinegar
3 tablespoons freshly grated Parmesan cheese

Place green and red onions and bay leaf in a flat microwave-safe serving dish. Toss with olive oil. Microwave on 100% (HIGH) 3 minutes. Stir. Microwave on 100% (HIGH) 2 to 3 minutes more or until onions are tender. Toss with vinegar and Parmesan cheese. This is best served at room temperature. Makes 4 to 6 servings.

Vegetables with Peanut Sauce

Gado Gado — Indonesia

A colorful combination of vegetables and eggs is served with the traditional Sati Peanut Sauce in Indonesia. You can use any vegetables that sound good to you. If this salad doesn't seem to fit what you would expect from the East Indies, just remember that Indonesia was ruled by the Dutch until 1945.

2 medium-size boiling potatoes

1/4 lb. carrots, thinly sliced diagonally

1/4 lb. green beans, stem ends removed

Banana or ti leaves, if desired

1/2 cucumber, peeled if desired, sliced

1 cup bean sprouts

2 hard-cooked eggs, cut in quarters

1 recipe Peanut Dipping Sauce, page 57

Shredded coconut to garnish

Prick potatoes 3 or 4 times with a fork. Place on a paper towel in microwave oven. Microwave on 100% (HIGH) 6 to 8 minutes or until tender, turning potatoes over after 3 minutes. Wrap tightly in foil and let stand 10 minutes. Place carrots in a medium-size microwave-safe bowl. Cover tightly. Microwave on 100% (HIGH) 2 to 4 minutes or until tender. Let stand 5 minutes. Place green beans in a medium-size microwave-safe bowl. Cover tightly. Microwave on 100% (HIGH) 1 to 2 minutes or just until tender. Cut potatoes in wedges. If desired, line a serving basket with banana leaves. Arrange cooked vegetables, cucumber, bean sprouts and eggs in serving basket. Garnish Peanut Dipping Sauce with shredded coconut and serve with salad. Makes 4 servings.

Salad with Bacon

Salad au Lard — France

French is usually considered such a beautiful language, but the American connotation of lard really catches your imagination!

1 small head chicory or curly endive, torn in bite-size pieces

4 strips bacon, finely chopped

3 tablespoons cider vinegar

Place chicory in a salad bowl. Spread bacon pieces in a flat microwave-safe dish. Cover with a paper towel. Microwave on 100% (HIGH) 2 to 4 minutes or until crisp. Quickly stir in vinegar and pour over chicory. Toss and serve at once. Makes 4 servings.

Vegetables with Peanut Sauce, above.

Spicy Cucumber Salad

Ajad — *Thailand*

Rice vinegar is a very mild vinegar available in many supermarkets in the oriental foods section. It needs very little oil to balance out the flavor if you are using it for a vinaigrette.

1 cup rice vinegar
3 tablespoons sugar
1 tablespoon finely chopped fresh cilantro
1/4 teaspoon dried red pepper flakes, crushed
1 large cucumber, peeled, thinly sliced
1/2 medium-size red onion, thinly sliced
1 medium-size carrot, peeled, thinly sliced
Black pepper to taste

In a medium-size microwave-safe bowl, combine vinegar and sugar. Microwave on 100% (HIGH) 3 minutes. Stir until sugar dissolves. Stir in cilantro and red pepper flakes. Let stand until room temperature. In a serving bowl, toss cucumber, onion and carrot with vinegar mixture. Season with black pepper. Refrigerate at least 2 hours or overnight. Makes 4 servings.

Caviatelli & Broccoli Salad

Insalata di Broccoli & Pasta — *Italy*

Caviatelli pasta looks like an oval shell, usually about one-half inch long. As pasta cooks best conventionally, I suggest you cook the caviatelli on the conventional range.

1/3 cup olive oil
1-1/2 cups fresh broccoli florets
1 garlic clove, minced
1 red bell pepper, cored, seeded
8 ozs. caviatelli or rotelli pasta, cooked, rinsed
1/4 cup white wine vinegar
1/3 cup freshly grated Parmesan cheese

In a large microwave-safe bowl, combine olive oil, broccoli and garlic. Cover tightly. Microwave on 100% (HIGH) 3 to 4 minutes or until broccoli is just slightly cooked, stirring after 2 minutes. Wrap bell pepper tightly in plastic wrap. Microwave on 100% (HIGH) 5 to 6 minutes or until completely soft. Let stand 10 minutes before unwrapping. Remove peel. Cut bell pepper in 1/4-inch slices. In a serving bowl, combine broccoli mixture, bell pepper, pasta, vinegar and Parmesan cheese. Serve at room temperature. Makes 4 to 6 servings.

Bulgar Salad

Tabbouleh — *Middle East*

Tabbouleh is a perfect picnic salad. It should be made ahead of time and it travels well. Bulgar can usually be purchased in health food stores if you can't find it in the supermarket.

1 cup bulgar wheat
1-1/2 cups water
1 cup chopped tomatoes
3 tablespoons chopped fresh mint
1/2 cup chopped fresh parsley
1/2 cup chopped green onions
1/2 cup fresh lemon juice
1/3 cup olive oil
Salt and black pepper to taste

In a microwave-safe bowl, combine bulgar and water. Microwave on 100% (HIGH) 4 to 5 minutes or just until water comes to a boil. Let stand 10 minutes. Drain well. In a serving bowl, toss bulgar, tomatoes, mint, parsley, green onions, lemon juice and olive oil. Season with salt and pepper. Refrigerate at least 1 hour to chill thoroughly. Makes 6 servings.

Bean Salad

Salata od Pasulja — *Hungary*

This salad would be perfect for a picnic. Use kidney beans or white northern beans if you prefer.

6 slices bacon
1 small onion, chopped
1 (20-oz.) can kidney beans, drained
3 hard-cooked eggs, diced
2 tablespoons finely chopped fresh parsley
2 tablespoons olive oil
1/4 to 1/2 teaspoon Hungarian paprika
1 lemon, cut in 6 wedges

Place bacon in a flat microwave-safe dish. Cover with a paper towel. Microwave on 100% (HIGH) 4 to 6 minutes or until crisp. Drain on paper towels. Stir onion into bacon fat. Microwave on 100% (HIGH) 2 to 3 minutes or until tender. Drain off fat. Crumble bacon. In a serving bowl, combine bacon, onion, beans, eggs, parsley, olive oil and paprika. Serve with lemon wedges. Makes 4 to 6 servings.

Pineapple Shrimp Fried Rice

Khow Pad Koong — *Thailand*

Fish sauce is a seasoning often used in oriental cooking. Its strong odor comes from fermented anchovies, fish and salt. Once blended with other ingredients, it produces a mild and pleasant flavor.

1 large pineapple
2 tablespoons vegetable oil
1/2 medium-size onion, chopped
3/4-lb. small shrimp, peeled, deveined
1 clove garlic, minced
4 cups cooked white long-grain rice
2 tablespoons fish sauce, if desired
2 teaspoons chopped fresh mint
1 green onion, finely chopped

Cut pineapple in half. Scoop out pulp, leaving 1 pineapple shell half intact. Chop enough pineapple pulp to measure 1 cup. Place oil and onion in a large flat-bottom microwave-safe dish. Microwave on 100% (HIGH) 2 minutes. Stir in shrimp and garlic. Microwave on 100% (HIGH) 1 to 2 minutes or until all shrimp are pink. Let stand, covered, 5 minutes. Stir in chopped pineapple pulp, rice, fish sauce, if desired, and mint. Spoon rice mixture into pineapple shell. Cover with plastic wrap. Microwave on 100% (HIGH) 4 to 5 minutes or until heated through. Sprinkle with green onion. Makes 4 to 6 servings.

Fast Rice & Cheese Salad

Risotto — *Italy / U. S. A.*

No respectable Italian cook would admit to using this recipe. But I find it a perfect way to use up leftover rice.

1/2 medium-size onion, chopped
2 tablespoons butter or margarine
2 cups cooked white short-grain rice
1/3 cup half and half
1/2 cup freshly grated Parmesan cheese

Place onion and butter in a medium-size microwave-safe bowl. Microwave on 100% (HIGH) 3 minutes. Stir in rice, half and half and Parmesan cheese. Cover tightly. Microwave on 100% (HIGH) 3 to 4 minutes or until hot. Makes 4 servings.

Seafood

The versatility of seafood is often overlooked. When you explore the cuisines of the world and see how each country takes the same types of seafood and adds their own flavorings and preparation methods, you will be amazed. For example we're familiar with the oyster stew so popular in the eastern part of the United States, but what about oysters cooked in the shell and served with champagne sauce or the German combination of cod and oysters. You have to agree that seafood is indeed versatile!

The perfect moistness of microwave cooking combined with the easy portion control of seafood makes shopping and cooking for two to twenty easy. Steaks and fillets by the pound or piece and seafood—fresh, frozen or canned—is easily accessible across our country.

In early Roman times the fish merchants were prevented by law from sitting down until all their fish were sold. This of course was to prevent them from selling spoiled fish due to the lack of refrigeration. The Spanish solved early refrigeration problems by heavily salting the cod they caught so that it could be transported into the interior cities. To prepare the salted cod, it was soaked in water for several hours to remove enough salt to make it edible. Cod was popular throughout Europe, so popular in fact that Escoffier, the famous French chef, wrote an entire book on ways to prepare it.

Most of the seafood eaten in China is the same as in the United States — tuna, shrimp, scallops and oysters to name a few of the most popular. Their simple, quick methods of preparation translate easily to the American palate. In China in ancient times as well as today, the quality and freshness of ingredients is critically important. The markets haul in large pots of water that hold live fish so it can be sold at its freshest and, due to the lack of refrigeration, last as long as possible.

Throughout all of Polynesia seafood caught off their extensive coastlines has been a mainstay in their diets. The most common way of cooking seafood there is in an open pit or steamed which produces a similar cooking effect as the microwave oven. They often wrap seafood along with other ingredients in banana or other leaves to keep the moistness in, the same as we use plastic wrap in the microwave oven.

World War II played a large part in opening up America to the versatility of seafood. The large number of soldiers in the South Pacific and Orient brought home ideas and tastes for seafood never before considered.

Anchovy Tomato Sandwich

Pan Bagna — *France*

This sandwich is traditionally served at room temperature, but I prefer it warm. Be sure not to overheat it!

1 long loaf soft-type French Bread, cut in half lengthwise
1/4 cup olive oil
1/8 teaspoon garlic powder
2 medium-size very ripe tomatoes, sliced
4 ozs. anchovy fillets
1 tablespoon capers, drained
1/4 cup chopped black olives

Sprinkle cut sides of bread with olive oil and garlic. Place tomatoes on bottom half of bread in a single layer. Top with anchovies, capers and olives. Cut in 4 to 6 pieces. Place pieces on a microwave-safe serving plate. Microwave on 100% (HIGH) 1 minute or just until bread is warm and soft. Makes 4 to 6 sandwiches.

Carp with Sour Cream

Karpfen mit Rahm — *Austria*

Cod can be substituted for the carp. I like to sprinkle a little paprika on top for some eye catching color.

4 new potatoes, thinly sliced
3 tablespoons butter or margarine
1 cup dairy sour cream
1-1/2 lbs. carp fillets
2 tablespoons dry bread crumbs

Place potatoes in a large flat-bottom microwave-safe dish. Dot with butter. Cover tightly. Microwave on 100% (HIGH) 4 to 6 minutes or until potatoes are tender. Spread 1/2 of sour cream over potatoes. Lay fish on potatoes. Spread remaining sour cream over fish. Sprinkle with bread crumbs. Re-cover and microwave on 100% (HIGH) 3 to 4 minutes or until fish is opaque. Let stand, covered, 5 minutes. Makes 4 servings.

Cod with Oysters from Hamburg

Hamburger Kabeljau mit Austern — *Germany*

When oysters are done, the edges will have a ruffled appearance. Overcooking will make them tough and difficult to chew.

1-1/2 lbs. cod fillets
1/4 teaspoon allspice
1 lemon, thinly sliced
1/2 cup dry white wine
1/4 cup bottled clam juice
1 tablespoon fine dry bread crumbs
Dash of nutmeg
12 oysters, shucked

Place fish in a large flat-bottom microwave-safe dish. Sprinkle with allspice. Reserve 2 lemon slices. Arrange remaining lemon slices over fish. Cover tightly. Microwave on 100% (HIGH) 5 to 7 minutes or until fish is opaque. Let stand, covered, 5 minutes. In a large microwave-safe bowl, combine reserved lemon slices, wine, clam juice, bread crumbs and nutmeg. Microwave on 100% (HIGH) 3 minutes or until mixture begins to boil. Add oysters. Cover tightly. Microwave on 100% (HIGH) 3 to 5 minutes or just until edges of oysters look ruffled. Spoon oysters and sauce over fish. Makes 4 servings.

Salmon Skewers

Northwestern U. S. A.

The northwestern part of America is well known for its bountiful seafood. I have never seen so much salmon as I saw at the famous Pike's Market in Seattle, Washington. Huge mounds of salmon packed in ice are just waiting to be purchased.

1 (2-lb.) salmon fillet
12 (8-inch) wooden skewers
1/4 cup butter or margarine, softened
2 tablespoons fresh lime juice
1 tablespoon chopped fresh tarragon or rosemary

Cut fish crosswise in 1-inch-wide strips. Thread fish strips onto skewers. Place in a large flat-bottom microwave-safe dish. In a small microwave-safe bowl, combine butter, lime juice and tarragon. Microwave on 100% (HIGH) 1-1/2 to 2 minutes or until butter melts. Stir well. Brush fish strips with butter mixture. Cover tightly. Microwave on 100% (HIGH) 2 to 3 minutes. Brush fish strips again with butter mixture. Re-cover and microwave on 100% (HIGH) 1 to 2 minutes more or until fish strips are opaque. Let stand, covered, 5 minutes. Makes 6 servings.

Salmon Steaks en Gelée

Saumon en Gelée *France*

Glistening orange salmon steaks are so elegant to serve and easy to prepare!

4 (6-oz.) salmon steaks, about 3/4-inch thick
1/2 cup dry white wine
1/2 teaspoon dried leaf tarragon
Green onion stems, black olives and pimiento to garnish

Gelée Glaze:
1 (.25-oz.) envelope unflavored gelatin
1 cup dry white wine
Assortment of lettuce
Lime twists to garnish

Place fish in a large flat-bottom microwave-safe dish. Pour wine over fish. Sprinkle with tarragon. Cover tightly with plastic wrap, pressing plastic wrap down so it rests on top of fish. Microwave on 100% (HIGH) 3 to 5 minutes or just until fish turns opaque. Let stand, covered, 5 minutes. Refrigerate salmon until cold, about 2 hours. To prepare gelée, in a small microwave-safe bowl, combine gelatin and wine. Let stand 5 minutes to soften gelatin. Microwave on 100% (HIGH) 3 minutes or until mixture comes to a boil. Stir until gelatin is dissolved. Cool gelée until syrupy, but not set. Place cold fish on a wire rack set on a baking sheet. Remove fish skin and gently clean off top. Spoon a thin layer of gelée over top and sides of fish. Cut green onion stems, olives and pimiento in thin strips. Arrange on top of gelée to garnish. Refrigerate fish 20 minutes or until gelée is set. Spoon remaining gelée over fish, completely covering garnish. If remaining gelée sets, microwave on 100% (HIGH) 10 to 20 seconds or just until warm. Serve salmon on lettuce. Garnish with lime twists. Makes 4 servings.

Swordfish with Oranges

Pesca con Naranja *Mexico*

Swordfish weighing over 200 pounds are caught off the western coast of Mexico. This cold dish can be served as a main dish or cut in bite-size pieces and served as an appetizer.

2 lbs. swordfish steaks
1/3 cup vegetable oil
1/3 cup fresh orange juice
1/3 cup cider vinegar
1 clove garlic, minced
2 tablespoons minced green onion
1 (2-oz.) can diced green chilies
Curly leaf lettuce
Orange slices

Lay fish in a large flat-bottom microwave-safe dish. Cover tightly. Microwave on 100% (HIGH) 5 to 7 minutes or until opaque. Let stand, covered, 5 minutes. To prepare marinade, in a small bowl, whisk oil, orange juice, vinegar, garlic, green onion and green chilies. If serving as an appetizer, cut fish in 1-1/2-inch cubes. Leave fish steaks whole if serving as a main dish. Pour marinade over fish. Re-cover and refrigerate 2 to 4 hours, gently stirring cubes or turning fish steaks over after 1 hour. Line a serving platter with lettuce. Place fish on lettuce and garnish with orange slices. Makes 6 to 8 servings.

Salmon Steaks en Gelée, above.

Fillet of Sole with Leeks

Filets de Sole au Poireaux — *Switzerland*

Saffron is usually thought of as a Spanish spice, essential to authentic paella. It is considered the most expensive herb and requires thousands of crocus to produce one pound. Its destinctive flavor and golden color add a special glow to foods.

3 medium-size leeks, cleaned
1/4 cup butter or margarine
1 cup champagne
Pinch saffron, finely crushed
1-1/2 lbs. sole fillets
2 tablespoons all-purpose flour
About 1 cup half and half
1 tablespoon red caviar

Thinly slice white part of leeks; discard green part. Place leeks in a medium-size flat-bottom microwave-safe dish. Dot with 2 tablespoons of butter. Cover tightly. Microwave on 100% (HIGH) 5 minutes, stirring once during cooking. Stir in champagne and saffron. Smooth leeks out flat. Lay fish on leeks. Cover tightly. Microwave on 100% (HIGH) 6 to 7 minutes or until fish is opaque. Let stand, covered, 5 minutes. To prepare sauce, in a small microwave-safe bowl, microwave remaining butter 15 to 20 seconds or until melted. Stir in flour. Microwave on 100% (HIGH) 30 seconds. Drain liquid from dish into a 2-cup glass measure. Add enough half and half to make 1-1/2 cups. Whisk liquid into butter mixture. Microwave on 100% (HIGH) 3 to 5 minutes or until mixture boils and starts to thicken. Remove fish and leeks to a serving platter. Pour sauce over fish and leeks. Sprinkle caviar over sauce. Makes 4 servings.

Sole with Grapes

Sole Veronique — *France*

Veronique *refers to the grapes added to a dish. This is a very elegant dish and perfect when you want to impress your dinner guests. Any kind of white fish fillets can be used in this recipe with great success.*

1/2 cup white wine
2 tablespoons chopped shallots
4 (4-oz.) sole fillets or 1-1/2 lbs. sole fillets
1/2 cup whipping cream
1 cup green seedless grapes
Salt and black pepper to taste

Place wine and shallots in a medium-size flat-bottom microwave-safe dish. Microwave on 100% (HIGH) 1 to 2 minutes or until shallots are tender. Place fish in dish. Cover tightly. Microwave on 100% (HIGH) 3 to 5 minutes or until fish is opaque. Let stand, covered, 5 minutes. Remove fish to a serving platter. Cover to keep warm. To prepare sauce, stir cream into liquid in dish. Cover tightly. Microwave on 100% (HIGH) 2 to 3 minutes or until mixture comes to a boil. Stir in grapes. Re-cover and microwave on 100% (HIGH) 1 to 2 minutes or until heated; do not cook grapes. Season with salt and pepper. Mix well. Spoon sauce over fish. Makes 4 servings.

Sole in Brie Sauce

Sole au Gratin — *France*

Au gratin *is a French term which applies to any dish made with a sauce and cheese. This loose translation is used so often in American cooking that the word* au gratin *is found in English dictionaries.*

1-1/2 lbs. sole fillets
2 tablespoons dry vermouth
1 tablespoon finely chopped fresh basil leaves or 1 teaspoon dried leaf basil
2 tablespoons butter or margarine
2 tablespoons all-purpose flour
3/4 cup chicken broth
1/4 cup whipping cream
2 ozs. Brie cheese, skin removed, finely chopped
4 ozs. snow crabmeat

Lay fish in a large flat-bottom microwave-safe dish. Sprinkle with vermouth and basil. Cover tightly. Microwave on 100% (HIGH) 4 to 5 minutes or until fish is opaque. Let stand, covered, 5 minutes. To make sauce, in a small microwave-safe bowl, microwave butter on 100% (HIGH) 15 to 30 seconds. Stir in flour. Microwave on 100% (HIGH) 30 seconds. Stir in chicken broth and cream. Microwave on 100% (HIGH) 3 to 4 minutes or until mixture starts to thicken. Stir in cheese until smooth. If necessary, microwave on 100% (HIGH) 1 minute to heat. In another small microwave-safe bowl, microwave crab on 100% (HIGH) 1 to 1-1/2 minutes or until warm. Remove fish to a serving platter. Pour sauce over fish. Break crab in small pieces and sprinkle over sauce. Makes 4 servings.

Baked Whole Snapper

Pesce Al Forno — *Italy*

The microwave oven is perfect for cooking a whole fish. The quick cooking assures an attractive fish with a wonderful fresh flavor.

1 (4- to 5-lb.) whole red snapper, cleaned
1/2 cup dry white wine
1 medium-size onion, thinly sliced
1 bunch fresh oregano
3 tablespoons butter or margarine, softened
2 tablespoons capers

Rinse fish well. Lay fish in a large flat-bottom microwave-safe dish. Pour wine over fish. Place onion and 3 sprigs of oregano inside cavity of fish. Tuck 3 sprigs of oregano under fish and lay 3 on top. Cover tightly. Microwave on 100% (HIGH) 10 minutes. Rotate dish one-half turn. Microwave on 100% (HIGH) 3 to 5 minutes more or until fish is opaque. Let stand, covered, 5 minutes. Remove fish to a serving platter. Cover to keep warm. To prepare sauce, stir butter and capers into liquid in dish. Microwave on 100% (HIGH) 3 to 4 minutes or until mixture boils. Spoon sauce over fish. Makes 6 to 8 servings.

Good Woman Sole

Fillets of Sole Bonne Femme *France*

Two sauces for one dish add that extra touch of French flavor, and as the title of this recipe implies, you'd have to be a "good woman" to go to all that trouble! Luckily the microwave oven makes it easy for a man or woman to be a great cook.

6 (6- to 8-oz.) sole fillets
1/4 cup plus 2 tablespoons butter or margarine
1/4 cup dry white wine
1/4 cup water
1 medium-size onion, thinly sliced
1 bay leaf
3 tablespoons all-purpose flour
Dash of cayenne pepper
1/4 cup half and half
4 ozs. fresh mushrooms, sliced
1/2 teaspoon fresh lemon juice
1/8 teaspoon paprika
1 recipe Quick Béarnaise Sauce, page 56

Lay fish in a large flat-bottom microwave-safe dish. Dot with 2 tablespoons of butter. Pour wine and water over fish. Arrange onion and bay leaf on fish. Cover tightly. Microwave on 100% (HIGH) 6 to 8 minutes or until fish is opaque. Let stand, covered, 5 minutes. To prepare white sauce, in a 2-cup glass measure, microwave 3 tablespoons of butter on 100% (HIGH) 1 minute or until melted. Stir in flour and cayenne pepper. Microwave on 100% (HIGH) 30 seconds. Add 1 cup of liquid from dish and half and half. Stir until well mixed. Microwave on 100% (HIGH) 3 to 4 minutes or until mixture begins to thicken. Cover and set aside. Place 1 tablespoon of butter, mushrooms, lemon juice and paprika in a small microwave-safe bowl. Cover tightly. Microwave on 100% (HIGH) 1-1/2 to 2 minutes or until mushrooms are tender. Stir to coat mushrooms. Remove fish to a microwave-safe serving platter. Pour white sauce over fish. Top with Quick Béarnaise Sauce, then mushrooms. To reheat, microwave on 100% (HIGH) 2 to 3 minutes or until hot. Makes 6 servings.

Cooking Tip:
Always place the thickest part of any food to be cooked toward the outside of the dish for more even cooking.

Fish with Paprika

Hal Paprikas *Hungary*

Paprika is made from ground sweet peppers or pimientos. Sweet Hungarian-type paprika can be used by the tablespoonful. The American type, used mostly for garnish, has a harsher flavor.

2 medium-size onions, thinly sliced
2 tablespoons butter or margarine
1 tablespoon Hungarian sweet paprika
Pinch red cayenne pepper
1-1/2 lbs. sole or sea bass fillets
Salt and black pepper to taste
3/4 cup dairy sour cream

Place onions in a large flat-bottom microwave-safe dish. Dot with butter and sprinkle with paprika and cayenne pepper. Cover tightly. Microwave on 100% (HIGH) 6 to 7 minutes or until onions are very tender, stirring once during cooking. Smooth onions out flat. Lay fish on onions. Season with salt and pepper. Cover tightly. Microwave on 100% (HIGH) 4 to 6 minutes or until fish is opaque. Let stand, covered, 5 minutes. Remove fish. Stir sour cream into onions. Place fish back on onions. Cover tightly. Microwave on 100% (HIGH) 1 to 2 minutes or until heated through. Makes 4 servings.

Steamed Fish

Li Yü *China*

The Chinese cut slashes in the side of the fish to let in the flavor. To serve, remove fish fillets by picking fish up by the tail. Insert a fork just under the skin at the tail and gently lift off fillet. Repeat on other side.

3 fresh or dried shitake mushrooms
1 cup water
1/4 cup soy sauce
1/2 cup chopped green onion
1/2 carrot, cut in julienne strips
1 red chili pepper, seeded, thinly sliced
1 tablespoon freshly grated orange peel
1 tablespoon shredded gingerroot
2 tablespoons vegetable oil
1 (2-lb.) whole red snapper

Place mushrooms and water in a small microwave-safe bowl. Cover tightly. Microwave on 100% (HIGH) 1 minute. Let stand 15 minutes. Drain mushrooms and thinly slice. In a medium-size microwave-safe bowl, combine mushrooms, soy sauce, green onion, carrot, chili pepper, orange peel, gingerroot and oil. Cover tightly. Microwave on 100% (HIGH) 1-1/2 to 2 minutes or until hot. Place fish on a microwave-safe serving platter. Spoon 1/2 of vegetable mixture inside cavity of fish. Cut 4 diagonal slashes on top side of fish. Spoon remaining vegetable mixture on fish. Cover tightly. Microwave on 100% (HIGH) 6 to 8 minutes or until fish is opaque. Let stand, covered, 5 minutes. Makes 4 servings.

Veracruz-Style Fish

Pescado Veracruz *Mexico*

Veracruz, Mexico has become famous for their tomato-sauced seafood. So much so that when you mention Veracruz and fish, you automatically know the fish has a tomato sauce.

1 tablespoon butter or margarine
1/2 cup chopped onion
1 clove garlic, minced
2 cups chopped peeled seeded tomatoes or 1 (24-oz.) can whole tomatoes, drained, chopped
1 (4-oz.) can diced Anaheim green chilies
1/2 teaspoon salt (omit if using canned tomatoes)
1/8 teaspoon black pepper
1 tablespoon fresh lime juice
1-1/2 lbs. red snapper fillets
Fresh cilantro sprigs and lemon and lime twists to garnish

To prepare sauce, place butter, onion and garlic in a large flat-bottom microwave-safe plate. Microwave on 100% (HIGH) 2 minutes. Stir in tomatoes, green chilies, salt, if using, pepper and lime juice. Cover tightly. Microwave on 100% (HIGH) 5 minutes. Lay fish in a single layer on sauce. Re-cover and microwave on 100% (HIGH) 5 to 8 minutes or until fish is opaque. Let stand, covered, 5 minutes. Garnish with cilantro and lemon and lime twists. Makes 4 servings.

Poached Red Fish with Avocado Sauce

Poisson Sarde Cuit avec la Sauce d'Avocat *Haiti*

French is the language of Haiti, even though the French formally withdrew over 100 years ago. Haitian cuisine has a French heritage with African and Caribbean overtones.

2 lbs. red snapper fillets
2 cups dry white wine
1 teaspoon dried leaf thyme
1 bay leaf
2 medium-size avocados
1 tablespoon olive oil
1 tablespoon chopped green onion
2 tablespoons fresh lime juice
1 small clove garlic, finely minced
1/4 teaspoon cayenne pepper
Salt to taste

Place fish in a large flat-bottom microwave-safe dish. Pour wine over fish. Sprinkle fish with thyme and add bay leaf. Cover tightly. Microwave on 100% (HIGH) 6 minutes. Rotate dish one-half turn. Microwave on 100% (HIGH) 3 to 5 minutes more or until fish is opaque. Let stand, covered, 5 minutes. To prepare sauce, peel and remove seed from avocado. Mash avocado in a small bowl. Stir in olive oil, green onion, lime juice, garlic and cayenne pepper. Season with salt. Remove fish to a serving platter and serve with sauce. Makes 4 servings.

Veracruz-Style Fish, above.

Shellfish Stew *(Photo on cover)*

Zarzuela *Spain*

Zarzuela *must be made with a large variety of seafood—use your imagination and whatever is available. The ingredient list of this recipe may be long, but the preparation time is quite short and manageable.*

1 large onion, chopped
4 medium-size tomatoes, seeded, chopped
1 clove garlic, minced
1/4 cup olive oil
1 lb. halibut or white fish, cut in cubes
1 lb. medium-size shrimp, peeled, deveined
1 dozen clams in shell
1 dozen mussels in shell
2 (1/2-lb.) lobster tails, cut in half lengthwise
1 (8-oz.) bottle clam juice
2 tablespoons fresh chopped parsley
3 tablespoons fresh lemon juice

In a very large microwave-safe dish, combine onion, tomatoes, garlic and olive oil. Cover tightly. Microwave on 100% (HIGH) 3 to 4 minutes or until onion is tender. Add fish, shrimp, clams, mussels, lobster tails and clam juice. Cover tightly. Microwave on 100% (HIGH) 5 to 8 minutes or until fish is opaque and clams and mussels open. Discard any clams or mussels that do not open. Sprinkle with parsley and lemon juice. Makes 4 servings.

Scallops in Wine

Coquilles Saint-Jaques *France*

The large scallop serving shells work great in the microwave oven. If you have none, use individual ramekins.

4 ozs. fresh mushrooms, sliced
1/2 medium-size onion, finely chopped
1/4 cup butter or margarine, softened
2 tablespoons all-purpose flour
1/2 cup dry white wine
1 lb. scallops
1/3 cup dry bread crumbs

Place mushrooms and onion in a medium-size flat-bottom microwave-safe dish. Dot with 2 tablespoons of butter. Cover tightly. Microwave on 100% (HIGH) 4 minutes or until onions are tender. In a 1-cup measure, dissolve flour in wine. Stir into mushroom mixture. Mix in scallops. Cover tightly. Microwave on 100% (HIGH) 2 minutes or just until scallops are opaque. Divide scallop mixture among 4 serving shells. In a small microwave-safe bowl, combine remaining butter and bread crumbs. Microwave on 100% (HIGH) 2 minutes. Sprinkle scallop mixture with buttered bread crumbs. Makes 4 servings.

Southern Shrimp Pie

U. S. A.

In the deep South spicy seafood is a specialty. Worcestershire sauce and hot-pepper sauce give these shrimp that characteristic Southern flavor.

1 cup chopped onions
1 tablespoon butter or margarine
1 (16-oz.) can tomatoes, undrained
1/2 cup tomato chili sauce
1 tablespoon Worcestershire sauce
2 to 4 dashes hot-pepper sauce
1/2 cup unsalted cracker crumbs
2 lbs. medium-size shrimp, peeled, deveined
1 tablespoon chopped fresh parsley

Place onions in a large microwave-safe bowl. Dot with butter. Microwave on 100% (HIGH) 3 minutes. Stir in tomatoes, chili sauce, Worcestershire sauce, hot-pepper sauce, cracker crumbs and shrimp. Spoon mixture into a 9-inch microwave-safe pie plate. Cover tightly. Microwave on 100% (HIGH) 5 minutes or until shrimp are bright pink. Let stand, covered, 5 minutes. Sprinkle with parsley. Makes 4 servings.

Shrimp with Tomato Sauce

Crevettes Grilles a la Kerkennaise — *Tunisia*

Tunisia was governed by the French from 1881 until 1956, so French influence on Tunisian cuisine is very strong. This recipe also has a Mediterranean feeling with the olive oil and tomato-base sauce.

2 lbs. medium-size shrimp, peeled, deveined
1/2 cup olive oil
3 large tomatoes, finely chopped
1/3 cup finely chopped fresh parsley
1 clove garlic, minced
1/2 teaspoon salt
1/2 teaspoon crushed red pepper flakes
1 lime, cut in 6 wedges

In a large microwave-safe bowl, toss shrimp with 1/4 cup of olive oil. Cover tightly. Microwave on 100% (HIGH) 3 minutes. Stir. Re-cover and microwave on 100% (HIGH) 2 to 4 minutes more or until all shrimp are pink. Let stand, covered, 5 minutes. To make dipping sauce, in a medium-size bowl, combine remaining olive oil, tomatoes, parsley, garlic, salt and red pepper flakes. Arrange shrimp on a large serving platter with lime wedges and serve with dipping sauce. Makes 6 servings.

Shrimp with Lobster

Camarao com Lagosta — *Brazil*

Shrimp and lobster are plentiful in the beautiful coastal cities of South America. I only wish the prices were as reasonable in the states! If you want to make the shrimp look like more, slice it in half lengthwise.

2 tablespoons olive oil
1 clove garlic, minced
1 green chili pepper, seeded, minced
1/2 cup prepared green chili sauce
2 (1/2-lb.) lobster tails, shells removed, cut in half crosswise
1 lb. large shrimp, peeled, deveined

In a large flat-bottom microwave-safe dish, combine olive oil, garlic, chili pepper and green chili sauce. Microwave on 100% (HIGH) 1 minute. Add lobster tails. Cover tightly. Microwave on 100% (HIGH) 1 minute. Stir in shrimp. Re-cover and microwave on 100% (HIGH) 2 to 4 minutes or just until all shrimp turn pink. Be careful not to overcook. Let stand, covered, 5 minutes. Makes 4 servings.

Lobster in Curry Sauce

Kari — *Malaysia*

Curry powder is a combination of several spices, usually cumin, coriander, ginger, cayenne pepper, black pepper and turmeric. The tumeric gives curry its yellow color.

4 (1/2-lb.) lobster tails, shells removed
3/4 cup butter or margarine, softened
1 tablespoon finely chopped green onion
2 teaspoons curry powder
1/4 cup dry white wine
1 cup Basic White Sauce, page 55
1/2 cup dairy sour cream
Salt and black pepper to taste
2 cups cooked white long-grain rice

Place lobster tails in a large flat-bottom microwave-safe dish. Cover tightly. Microwave on 100% (HIGH) 3 to 4 minutes or just until lobster meat is opaque. Let stand, covered, 5 minutes. To make sauce, in a medium-size microwave-safe bowl, combine butter, green onion and curry powder. Microwave on 100% (HIGH) 3 minutes or until butter melts. Stir in wine, Basic White Sauce and sour cream. Season with salt and pepper. Mix well. Place lobster tails on rice and pour sauce over lobster tails. Makes 4 servings.

Poultry

Chicken seems to be the most universal meat. It takes very little space or food to produce it, and I haven't found any religious taboos. After the depression in America, people were promised a chicken in every pot and at that time a special Sunday supper was probably boiled chicken and dumplings.

In France many of the peasant chicken dishes like *pot au feu* have been elevated to classic heights by its great chefs. In fact the French word for chicken breast is *supremes*. Cooking simple things exceptionally well has been the French method. Historically, the method chosen for cooking a chicken depended on the age which indicates tenderness of the bird. A young chick could be sauteed while an old rooster would be stewed. The microwave oven with its moist method of cooking is perfect for any age bird. Luckily for the cook, chicken and turkey of excellent quality are widely available. It's hard to imagine how often you would cook poultry if you had to kill and clean it first!

In the United States chicken and turkey are the fowl of choice and availability with duck and goose showing up for special occasions or if you hunt them yourself. In Spain many types of wild game are available in the markets—pheasant, quail, pigeon and even owl. Partridge is often substituted for chicken in recipes.

Chicken has such a mild bland flavor that it can be curried as in Indian foods, combined in *mole* (with chocolate) in Mexican foods, encased in *bows* as in Chinese food or simmered in wine à la French *coq au vin*.

Chicken with Olives

Poulat aux Olives Farcies — *Tunisia*

The early French influence in this Mediterrean country shows in the title of this recipe, but the ingredients are definitely native. Olives are a very important part of the economy as well as the cuisine.

8 small new potatoes, peeled
1 teaspoon ground cumin
1/2 teaspoon paprika
2 tablespoons butter or margarine, softened
1-1/2 medium-size onions, minced
1 clove garlic, minced
1 lb. boneless skinned chicken breasts, cut in 1-inch cubes
1/2 cup minced pimiento-stuffed green olives
1/4 teaspoon black pepper
1/4 teaspoon crushed dried red pepper flakes

Place potatoes in a medium-size microwave-safe bowl. Cover tightly. Microwave on 100% (HIGH) 8 to 10 minutes or until tender. Let stand, covered, 5 minutes. In a large microwave-safe bowl, combine cumin, paprika, butter, onions and garlic. Cover tightly. Microwave on 100% (HIGH) 3 to 4 minutes or until onions are tender. Stir in chicken, olives and black and red pepper flakes. Re-cover and microwave on 100% (HIGH) 6 to 8 minutes or until chicken is tender, stirring twice during cooking. Gently mix in hot potatoes. Makes 4 servings.

Chicken with Mushrooms & Tomatoes

Pollo con Funghi e Pomodoro — *Italy*

Mushrooms, onions and tomatoes seem to be a common combination in all of the Mediterrean countries. This dish happens to be from Italy.

3 tablespoons butter or margarine
1 medium-size onion, thinly sliced
8 ozs. fresh mushrooms, cut in quarters
1 (6-oz.) can tomato paste
1 tablespoon freshly chopped basil or 1-1/2 teaspoons dried leaf basil
1/2 cup dry white wine
6 (4-oz.) boneless skinned chicken breasts

In a large flat-bottom microwave-safe dish, microwave butter on 100% (HIGH) 30 seconds or until melted. Add onion and mushrooms. Cover tightly. Microwave on 100% (HIGH) 2 to 3 minutes or until onions are tender. In a small bowl, combine tomato paste, basil and wine. Stir into mushroom mixture. Microwave on 100% (HIGH) 2 minutes. Place chicken in sauce, coating both sides of chicken. Cover tightly. Microwave on 70% (MEDIUM-HIGH) 12 to 15 minutes or until chicken is no longer pink in center. Let stand, covered, 5 minutes. Makes 4 to 5 servings.

Chicken in Spicy Sauce

Pollo Mole *Mexico*

Mole *is an unusual combination of tomato sauce and spices with a small amount of chocolate added to smooth out the flavor. For the best flavor make this a day ahead and reheat it in the microwave oven just before serving.*

1 (1-oz.) square unsweetened chocolate
1 cup tomato-base taco sauce
1/4 cup dark raisins
1/8 teaspoon ground cinnamon
1/8 teaspoon ground cloves
1 clove garlic, minced
3 lbs. chicken pieces
1/2 cup slivered almonds
1/4 cup sliced green onions

To prepare sauce, in a large microwave-safe bowl, microwave chocolate on 100% (HIGH) 20 seconds. Touch chocolate to see if it has melted. If necessary, microwave on 100% (HIGH) in 10 second increments until just melted, stirring during cooking. Stir in taco sauce, raisins, cinnamon, cloves and garlic. Arrange chicken pieces in a single layer in a large flat-bottom microwave-safe dish. Coat each piece with sauce. Cover tightly. Microwave on 100% (HIGH) 10 minutes. Brush sauce on chicken again. Microwave on 100% (HIGH) 8 to 10 minutes or until chicken is no longer pink in center. Let stand, covered, 10 minutes. Place almonds on a paper towel in microwave oven. Microwave on 100% (HIGH) 1 to 3 minutes or until almonds are very hot—do not let them burn. Sprinkle almonds and green onion over chicken. Makes 4 to 6 servings.

Spicy Chicken with Cashews

Kung Pao Chi *China*

This is one of the spiciest chicken dishes! Be sure not to eat the chili pieces unless you have a mouth of steel.

1 tablespoon cornstarch
1/4 cup soy sauce
4 (4-oz.) chicken breasts, cut in bite-size pieces
1 tablespoon sugar
1 teaspoon minced gingerroot
1 clove garlic, minced
1 tablespoon vegetable oil
1 teaspoon sesame oil
3 to 5 dried red chili peppers, crushed
1/2 cup whole cashew nuts

In a large bowl, dissolve cornstarch in soy sauce. Stir in chicken, sugar, gingerroot and garlic. Let stand 30 minutes, stirring twice during standing time. In a large microwave-safe bowl, combine vegetable oil, sesame oil and chili peppers. Microwave on 100% (HIGH) 2 minutes. Pour chicken mixture into chili peppers. Stir. Cover tightly. Microwave on 100% (HIGH) 3 to 4 minutes, stirring twice during cooking. Spoon onto serving a platter and sprinkle with cashews. Makes 4 servings.

Haitian-Style Chicken

Poulet a l'Haitienne *Haiti*

Serve this savory chicken on rice so you can be sure to taste the sauce. The fresh lime juice squeezed in at the end is important for that fresh flavor.

1/4 cup olive oil
2 cloves garlic, minced
2 teaspoons curry powder
3 medium-size onions, thinly sliced
2 lbs. boneless skinned chicken breast, cut in 2-inch cubes
1/8 teaspoon crushed saffron
1 teaspoon salt, if desired
1-1/2 teaspoons crushed red pepper flakes
3/4 cup chicken broth
2 tablespoons light rum
1 lime

In a small bowl, combine olive oil, garlic and curry powder. Arrange onions in a large microwave-safe dish. Pour seasoned olive oil over onions and toss. Cover tightly. Microwave on 100% (HIGH) 6 to 7 minutes or until onions are tender, stirring twice during cooking. Stir in chicken. Cover tightly. Microwave on 100% (HIGH) 8 to 10 minutes, stirring during cooking to separate chicken. Stir in chicken broth, saffron, salt, if desired, and red pepper flakes. Cover tightly. Microwave on 70% (MEDIUM-HIGH) 10 to 12 minutes or until chicken is tender. Stir in rum. Squeeze lime juice over top. Makes 4 to 6 servings.

Marinated Chicken

Gai Yang *Thailand*

Thai cuisine shows the influence of its neighboring countries, China and India. You will often find Indian curry used in recipes like this one.

3 lbs. chicken pieces
3/4 cup soy sauce
1/4 cup water
2 tablespoons chopped fresh cilantro
1 tablespoon curry powder
3 or 4 cloves garlic, minced
2 tablespoons sugar
1 tablespoon finely chopped gingerroot

Remove any excess fat from chicken. To prepare marinade, in a large flat-bottom microwave-safe dish, combine soy sauce, water, cilantro, curry powder, garlic, sugar and gingerroot. Place chicken in marinade, skin side up. Cover tightly. Refrigerate 2 hours. Microwave chicken and marinade on 100% (HIGH) 10 minutes. Rotate dish one-half turn. Microwave on 100% (HIGH) 10 to 12 minutes more or until chicken is no longer pink in center. If desired, broil chicken under a preheated broiler about 5 minutes to crisp skin. Makes 6 servings.

Chicken with Wine

Coq au Vin — *France*

This classic French poultry dish is one whose name is instantly familiar, but the actual dish is not often served due to the length of preparation time. In French kitchens this dish would be partially prepared and left to marinate in the refrigerator overnight. The potatoes would be cooked and added the next day. This microwave version is just as tasty and much quicker to prepare.

6 slices bacon, diced
3 lbs. chicken pieces
4 ozs. fresh mushrooms
8 small onions, peeled
8 small new potatoes, cut in half
1 clove garlic, minced
3 tablespoons all-purpose flour
1 teaspoon salt
1/2 teaspoon dried leaf thyme
1 cup Burgundy wine
1/2 cup condensed chicken broth, undiluted
Chopped fresh parsley

Place bacon in a large flat-bottom microwave-safe dish. Cover with a paper towel. Microwave on 100% (HIGH) 5 minutes or until crisp. Drain on a paper towel and crumble. Place chicken pieces in dish. Turn and coat pieces with bacon fat. Cover tightly. Microwave on 100% (HIGH) 10 minutes. Turn pieces over. Microwave on 100% (HIGH) 3 to 5 minutes more or until chicken is no longer pink in center. Remove chicken to a large dish. Cover and keep warm. In same dish, place mushrooms, onions, potatoes and garlic. Cover tightly. Microwave on 100% (HIGH) 6 minutes. Let stand, covered, 5 minutes. Remove vegetables to plate with chicken. Re-cover and keep warm. Stir flour, salt and thyme into liquid in dish. Microwave on 100% (HIGH) 2 minutes. Stir well. Stir in wine and chicken broth. Microwave on 100% (HIGH) 4 to 6 minutes or until mixture comes to a boil and begins to thicken, stirring frequently during cooking. Return chicken and vegetables to dish. Turn to coat with wine mixture. Cover tightly. Microwave on 70% (MEDIUM-HIGH) 15 minutes. Sprinkle with bacon and parsley. Makes 4 servings.

Cooking Tip:

Themometers made for the microwave oven are a useful accessory, especially when cooking large pieces of meat or poultry.

Chicken Enchiladas

Enchiladas con Pollo — *Mexico*

This combination of chicken, sour cream and green chilies is very popular in the southwestern part of the United States. It has been Americanized by serving the beans on top of the enchiladas.

2 cups shredded Cheddar cheese (8 ozs.)
1-3/4 cups chopped cooked chicken
1 cup dairy sour cream
1 (4-oz.) can chopped green chilies, undrained
10 (8-inch) flour tortillas
1 (16-oz.) can refried beans
1 (1.5-oz.) pkg. enchilada sauce seasoning mix

To prepare filling, in a medium-size bowl, combine 1-1/2 cups of cheese, chicken, 1/2 cup of sour cream and green chilies. Spoon 1/4 cup of filling down center of each tortilla. Roll tortillas up, jelly-roll style. Place seam-side-down in an 11'' x 7'' microwave-safe dish. Cover tightly. Microwave on 100% (HIGH) 5 minutes. In a small bowl, combine remaining sour cream, beans and seasoning mix. Spread evenly over rolled tortillas. Re-cover and microwave on 100% (HIGH) 3 to 5 minutes or until heated through. Sprinkle with remaining cheese. Makes 4 to 6 servings.

Sweet & Sour Marinated Chicken

Tien Swan Jiang Se Gee — *China — Hunan*

This spicy dish can be served warm with rice or cooled and served with wooden picks as an appetizer.

4 (4-oz.) chicken breasts
1-1/2 tablespoons minced gingerroot
2 tablespoons cider vinegar
2 teaspoons sugar
1/2 teaspoon salt
1/2 teaspoon sesame oil

Place chicken in a medium-size microwave-safe dish. Cover tightly. Microwave on 100% (HIGH) 6 to 8 minutes. Let stand, covered, 5 minutes. Remove skin and cut chicken in 1-inch squares. In a large bowl, mix gingerroot, vinegar, sugar, salt and sesame oil. Stir in chicken pieces. Makes 4 to 6 servings.

Boiled Chicken Dinner

Canada

This is a typical Sunday dinner for a Canadian family. Originally a stewing hen would be cut up and this moist method of cooking would tenderize it. The original tenderizing cooking process is not necessary today, but the long slow cooking blends the flavors beautifully.

1/4 lb. salt pork, diced
1 medium-size onion, sliced
2 stalks celery, diced
5 lbs. chicken pieces
1 cup water
2 bay leaves
1 teaspoon salt
1/2 teaspoon dried leaf thyme
1 small green cabbage, cut in 8 wedges
1 lb. green beans, trimmed
6 boiling potatoes, peeled, cut in quarters
6 carrots, peeled, thinly sliced
6 boiling onions

In a large microwave-safe dish, combine salt pork, onion slices and celery. Cover tightly. Microwave on 100% (HIGH) 5 minutes. Add chicken, water, bay leaves, salt and thyme. Re-cover and microwave on 100% (HIGH) 10 minutes. Rearrange chicken pieces. Re-cover and microwave on 50% (MEDIUM) 20 minutes. Add cabbage, green beans, potatoes, carrots and boiling onions. Re-cover and microwave on 100% (HIGH) 10 minutes. Rotate dish one-half turn. Microwave on 100% (HIGH) 10 minutes more or until vegetables are tender. Makes 6 servings.

Country Chicken Sandwich

Panino Pollo Rustice — *Italy*

Panino *is the Italian word for sandwich, derived from* pane *which means bread.* Panini *(meaning more than one) are made from any combination of ingredients and are considered the fast food of Italy.*

3 (4-oz.) boneless skinned chicken breasts
Salt and black pepper to taste
1 clove garlic, minced
1/4 cup olive oil
2 tablespoons white wine vinegar
4 Italian bread rolls, split
Dijon-style mustard
4 slices provolone cheese
1 recipe Bell Pepper Salad, page 65

Place chicken in a medium-size flat-bottom microwave safe dish. Season with salt and pepper. Cover tightly. Microwave on 100% (HIGH) 5 minutes. Rotate dish one-half turn. Microwave on 100% (HIGH) 1 to 2 minutes more or until no longer pink in center. Cut chicken in bite-size pieces. In a medium-size bowl, toss chicken with garlic, oil and vinegar. Spread rolls with mustard. Spoon chicken mixture onto bottom halves. Top each with a slice of provolone cheese and Bell Pepper Salad. Makes 4 sandwiches.

Chicken Stuffed with Spinach & Pine Nuts

Pollo di Spinaci — *Italy*

This dish is served cold for lunch or a light supper. When sliced the colorful filling makes for a beautiful display on the serving plate.

4 (4-oz.) boneless skinned chicken breasts, pounded flat
2 tablespoons Dijon-style mustard
4 ozs. provolone cheese, thinly sliced
1 tablespoon olive oil
1/4 cup pine nuts, chopped
1 clove garlic, minced
1 cup chopped fresh spinach
1 teaspoon dried leaf oregano

Spread each flattened chicken breast with mustard. Cover with cheese. In a microwave-safe glass pie plate, combine olive oil, pine nuts and garlic. Microwave on 100% (HIGH) 2 minutes. Stir in spinach and oregano. Cover tightly. Microwave on 100% (HIGH) 1 to 2 minutes or just until spinach is wilted. Spoon spinach mixture in strips along 1 edge of chicken breasts. Roll chicken up, jelly-roll style. Wrap each roll tightly in plastic wrap. Place rolls on a large flat microwave-safe plate. Microwave on 100% (HIGH) 6 to 10 minutes or until chicken is opaque. Let stand 10 minutes. Refrigerate wrapped until cold or overnight. To serve, unwrap and slice in 1/2-inch thick rounds. Makes 4 servings.

Steamed Whole Chicken

Ching Tsen Chwan Gee — *China — Szechaun*

Chicken is often expensive in China, so it is always prepared and cooked with great care.

1 (3-lb.) whole chicken
3 tablespoons soy sauce
2 tablespoons chopped green onion
1 tablespoon finely chopped gingerroot
1 tablespoon dry sherry

Place chicken in a deep medium-size microwave-safe dish. In a 2-cup measure, mix soy sauce, green onion, gingerroot and sherry. Brush cavity and outside of chicken with soy sauce mixture. Cover tightly. Microwave on 100% (HIGH) 10 minutes. Brush with any remaining sauce. Cover tips of wings and legs with small pieces of foil to prevent overcooking. Re-cover and microwave on 100% (HIGH) 10 to 12 minutes more. Let stand, covered, 10 minutes. Makes 4 servings.

Fresh fruit; Chicken Stuffed with Spinach & Pine Nuts, above.

Chicken & Ham Omelet

Bark Dow Dan *China*

The term omelet in Chinese cooking doesn't refer to a breakfast meal. Cooked eggs are often added to rice or meat and vegetable dishes for color and flavor.

1 tablespoon vegetable oil
1 medium-size onion, thinly sliced
1 cup diced cooked chicken
1/2 cup diced ham
6 fresh mushrooms, thinly sliced
1/2 cup bean sprouts
1/2 cup green peas
1/4 cup soy sauce
1/4 cup dry sherry
3 eggs
3 tablespoons water
1 cup chicken stock
1/4 cup ketchup
1 tablespoon cornstarch

Lightly grease an 8-inch-round microwave-safe glass cake dish. In a large microwave-safe bowl, toss oil and onion. Cover tightly. Microwave on 100% (HIGH) 2 to 3 minutes or until onion is tender. Stir in chicken, ham, mushrooms, bean sprouts, peas, soy sauce and sherry. Re-cover and microwave on 100% (HIGH) 2 to 3 minutes or until heated. In a small bowl, mix eggs and water. Pour into greased cake dish. Microwave on 100% (HIGH) 2 to 3 minutes or until set. Eggs should resemble a very flat pancake. To prepare sauce, in a 2-cup glass measure, combine chicken stock, catsup and cornstarch. Microwave on 100% (HIGH) 3 to 5 minutes or until mixture comes to a boil and is slightly thickened. To assemble dish, mound meat mixture in center of a serving plate. Top with egg omelete and pour sauce over top. Cut in wedges to serve. Makes 4 servings.

Ground Nut Stew

Nikatse Nkwa — *Africa*

Because Africa has had so many different countries colonizing it, the food is hard to place and determine exactly if it is truly native or imported. This stew uses ingredients commonly found throughout the continent.

6 lbs. chicken pieces
2 medium-size onions, chopped
2 medium-size sweet potatoes, peeled, cut in 1-inch cubes
2 cloves garlic, minced
1 tablespoon chili powder
1/2 teaspoon ground ginger
1 teaspoon salt
1 cup water
1 (6-oz.) can tomato paste
1-1/2 cups finely chopped peanuts
6 hard-cooked eggs
3 cups cooked white long-grain rice

Place chicken pieces in a large flat-bottom microwave-safe dish. Cover tightly. Microwave on 100% (HIGH) 10 minutes. Rearrange, turning over and exchanging center pieces with outside pieces. Re-cover and microwave on 100% (HIGH) 8 to 12 minutes more or until chicken is no longer pink in center. Remove chicken from dish. Cover to keep warm. Stir onions, sweet potatoes, garlic, chili, ginger and salt into juices in dish. Cover tightly. Microwave on 100% (HIGH) 5 to 7 minutes or until potatoes are tender. Stir in water, tomato paste and peanuts. Return chicken to dish. Re-cover and microwave on 100% (HIGH) 15 minutes to blend flavors. To serve, place a hard-cooked egg on each plate and cover with rice. Spoon chicken and sauce over rice. Makes 6 servings.

Chicken & Pork Stew

Adobo — *Philippines*

Philippine cuisine shows the cultural influence of several countries, including the United States, China and Spain. Serve this with rice if you like.

1 lb. boneless pork, cut in 1-inch cubes
1 lb. boneless skinned chicken, cut in 1-inch cubes
2 tablespoons olive oil
2 cloves garlic, minced
1/2 cup chicken stock
1/4 cup cider vinegar
1/4 cup soy sauce
1 teaspoon salt
1/2 teaspoon black pepper

Place pork in a medium-size flat-bottom microwave-safe dish. Cover tightly. Microwave on 100% (HIGH) 5 minutes. Stir in chicken, olive oil and garlic. Re-cover and microwave on 100% (HIGH) 5 minutes. Add chicken bouillon, vinegar, soy sauce, salt and pepper. Cover tightly. Microwave on 50% (MEDIUM) 12 to 15 minutes or until chicken and pork are tender. Makes 6 servings.

Couscous

Couscous — *Morocco*

Couscous is a dish of chicken or lamb and vegetables served on top of cooked cracked wheat. It is usually very spicy and the exact ingredients depend on which country is serving it. It is commonly found in those countries along the north coast of Africa.

1 cup dark raisins
3 lbs. chicken pieces
3 large onions, minced
2 medium-size carrots, peeled, thinly sliced
1/4 cup butter or margarine, softened
3 medium-size tomatoes, seeded, cut in cubes
2 cups canned garbanzo beans (chick peas) with juice
1/2 teaspoon ground cinnamon
1/2 teaspoon salt
1/2 teaspoon black pepper
1/4 teaspoon saffron
3 cups cooked couscous

In a small bowl, cover raisins with warm water. Arrange chicken pieces in a large deep microwave-safe dish. Sprinkle onions and carrots on chicken. Dot with butter. Cover tightly. Microwave on 100% (HIGH) 10 to 15 minutes or until chicken is no longer pink in center. Drain raisins. In a large bowl, combine raisins, tomatoes, garbanzo beans, cinnamon, salt, pepper and saffron. Pour over chicken. Re-cover and microwave on 100% (HIGH) 8 to 10 minutes or until very hot, stirring once during cooking. Mound couscous on a large serving platter. Arrange chicken and vegetables around edge of couscous. Makes 6 servings.

Currant-Ginger Duck

U. S. A.

My dad is a duck hunter, which means lots of duck in the freezer. If you prefer to cut out the breast and only cook it, you can. But here is a recipe for a whole duck.

1 (4- to 5-lb.) fresh or frozen duck, thawed if frozen
1 slice lemon
1 slice onion
1 cup red currant jelly
1 tablespoon soy sauce
1 teaspoon minced gingerroot
1 tablespoon dry sherry

Clean duck and pat dry. Place lemon and onion in cavity of duck. Tie legs together with cotton string and tuck wings under back. Place on a microwave-safe roasting rack set in a microwave-safe dish. To prepare glaze, in a small microwave-safe bowl, combine jelly, soy sauce, gingerroot and sherry. Microwave on 100% (HIGH) 30 to 60 seconds or until melted. Stir. Brush glaze on duck. Microwave duck on 100% (HIGH) 14 minutes. Brush more glaze in duck. Microwave on 100% (HIGH) 14 to 20 minutes more or until a microwave-safe thermometer pushed into thickest part of breast registers about 180F (80C). Prick skin to let fat run out. Cover duck with foil and let stand 10 minutes before carving. Makes 4 servings.

Capon with Chestnut Dressing

U. S. A.

Chestnuts are a favorite holiday nut. When cooked they are soft and their mild flavor goes well with savory or sweet flavorings.

1 (5-lb.) capon, cleaned
1/2 cup butter or margarine, softened
1/4 teaspoon Kitchen Bouquet
2 tablespoons dry sherry

Chestnut Stuffing:
1/2 medium-size onion, chopped
1/4 cup butter or margarine, softened
2 ozs. fresh mushrooms, thinly sliced
1 stalk celery, chopped
2 cups dry bread cubes
1 (15-oz.) can chestnuts, drained, or 3/4 lb. chestnuts, shelled
1/2 teaspoon salt
1/4 teaspoon dried leaf tarragon
1/4 teaspoon dried leaf basil
1/2 cup chicken stock

Prepare Chestnut Stuffing. Fill cavitiy of capon with stuffing. Place capon in a medium-size microwave-safe dish. In a 2-cup glass measure, combine butter, Kitchen Bouquet and sherry. Microwave on 100% (HIGH) 1 minute or until butter melts. Brush capon with butter mixture. Cover tightly. Microwave on 100% (HIGH) 35 to 40 minutes or until capon is tender, basting with butter mixture every 10 minutes. Makes 4 servings.

Chesnut Stuffing:
In a medium-size microwave-safe bowl, combine onion and butter. Cover tightly. Microwave on 100% (HIGH) 2 to 3 minutes or until onion is tender. Stir in mushrooms and celery. Re-cover and microwave on 100% (HIGH) 2 to 3 minutes or until vegetables are tender. Stir in bread crumbs, chestnuts, salt, tarragon, basil and chicken stock. Makes about 3 cups.

Turkey Vegetable Stir-Fry

U. S. A.

Turkey is one of the few original American foods. Luckily it is abundant and has a very mild flavor that combines well with more exotic flavorings. The Chinese cooking method of stir-fry works perfectly to combine western ingredients with eastern techniques.

1 lb. boneless turkey breast, thinly sliced
1 medium-size onion, thinly sliced
2 cups broccoli flowerets
1 cup thinly-sliced carrots
1/2 medium-size green bell pepper, thinly sliced
1 (16-oz.) can crushed tomatoes with juice
1 teaspoon dried leaf thyme
1/4 teaspoon ground ginger
2 tablespoons soy sauce

Place turkey slices in a large microwave-safe casserole dish. Cover tightly. Microwave on 100% (HIGH) 3 minutes. Stir to separate turkey slices. Re-cover and microwave on 100% (HIGH) 3 to 4 minutes more or until turkey slices are no longer pink. Stir in onion, broccoli, carrots and green pepper. Re-cover and microwave on 100% (HIGH) 5 minutes. Stir in tomatoes with juice, thyme, ginger and soy sauce. Re-cover and microwave on 100% (HIGH) 3 to 5 minutes or until hot. Makes 4 to 6 servings.

Meats

The United States is the beef capital of the world. Produced in huge quantities and of excellent quality, no other country consumes as much per capita as we do. In most countries around the world, beef is a luxury, saved for special occasions or stretched with vegetables like the stir-fry methods of the Orient.

In European countries like Spain and Italy, beef is not plentiful and it is slaughtered at a young age, so the cuts of beef are smaller in comparison to those in the United States. Lambs, pigs and goats are sent to market at a young age so they will be tender and flavorful. Dishes such as braised lamb tongue from France and pickled pigs feet were developed to utilize all of a scarce product and became delicacies. The microwave doesn't do well on either, so you won't find them included here!

Pork is considered a versatile and economical meat by the Chinese. They have hundreds of different ways to prepare it and they use every part from the tenderloin to the knuckles. Fresh pork called *schwein* in German, probably where our word swine came from, is one of their most popular meats. They produce large quantities of tasty sausages, ham and bacon. Italian prosciutto ham is well known as a delicacy.

Lamb historically has been popular in the Middle East where *shish kebabs* originated, but now are an American barbecue item. The term barbecue has one of two origins. The most widely accepted is from the Spanish word *barbacoa* which describes a lattice made of sticks that early explorers saw native Central American Indians cooking on. The second definition says the word comes from the French word *de barbe a'queue* meaning cooking the whole animal from "whiskers to tail" over a fire. While you can't barbecue with a microwave oven, it can help with barbecuing long-cooking meats such as ribs. By precooking them in the microwave oven and then completing over the coals for that wonderful flavor, you save time and moisture. A large variety of barbecue sauces can be made with the help of the microwave oven too.

Spicy Beef for Tortillas

Tortillas con Picadillo — *Mexico*

Picadillo *is kind of a "catch-all" ground meat and tomato dish. It is served as a filling for tacos or tostados, or it could be used to fill enchiladas or tamales. I like to serve it rolled in soft flour tortillas.*

1/2 cup slivered blanched almonds
1 lb. ground beef or pork
1 medium-size onion, finely chopped
1 clove garlic, minced
1/2 cup dark raisins
1 (16-oz.) can tomatoes, drained, chopped
1 teaspoon ground cinnamon
1/4 teaspoon ground cumin
1 teaspoon salt
1/4 teaspoon black pepper
2 tablespoons cider vinegar
12 (8-inch) flour tortillas
4 cups shredded lettuce
2 cups shredded Cheddar cheese (8 ozs.)

Place almonds on a paper towel in microwave oven. Microwave on 100% (HIGH) 2 to 3 minutes or until they begin to sizzle. In a large microwave-safe dish, combine ground beef, onion and garlic. Microwave on 100% (HIGH) 3 minutes. Stir to break up beef. Microwave on 100% (HIGH) 2 minutes more or until beef is no longer pink. Stir in raisins, tomatoes, cinnamon, cumin, salt, pepper and vinegar. Cover tightly. Microwave on 100% (HIGH) 5 to 7 minutes or until hot, stirring once during cooking. Place tortillas in plastic bag on a paper towel in microwave oven. Microwave on 100% (HIGH) 30 to 45 seconds or just until heated. Invite guests to spoon beef mixture down center of tortillas. Top with lettuce and cheese. Fold sides over to enclose filling. Makes 12 filled tortillas.

Cooking Tip:
The microwave oven is a great addition to the barbecue. Next time barbecue twice as much as you need, freeze half and use the microwave oven to defrost and reheat for excellent just-barbecued flavor without the fuss.

Yogurt Kabobs

Yogurtlu Kebap — *Turkey*

Even if you don't understand the Turkish language, you could probably guess what this dish is! The meatball mixture is great for an appetizer—just make the balls about one and one-half inches in diameter.

3/4 lb. ground beef
1/2 cup cooked white long-grain rice
1/2 medium-size onion, minced
2 teaspoons chopped fresh mint
2 teaspoons chopped fresh parsley
1/2 teaspoon salt
1/4 teaspoon allspice
1/4 teaspoon black pepper
2 tablespoons olive oil
1/4 cup finely chopped green onions
4 pita bread rounds, cut in half

Yogurt Sauce:
3 medium-size zucchini, coarsely chopped
2 medium-size tomatoes, coarsely chopped
2 cups plain yogurt
1 tablespoon chopped fresh mint

Prepare Yogurt Sauce. To prepare meatballs, in a medium-size bowl, combine ground beef, rice, onion, mint, parsley, salt, allspice, pepper and olive oil. Mix well. Shape in 16 egg-shape meatballs. Arrange in a single layer in a medium-size flat-bottom microwave-safe dish. Cover loosely with waxed paper. Microwave on 100% (HIGH) 3 minutes. Gently turn meatballs over. Microwave on 100% (HIGH) 3 to 5 minutes more or until meatballs are no longer pink in center. Gently mix hot meatballs into yogurt sauce. Spoon onto a serving platter. Sprinkle with green onions. Place pita bread halves in a plastic bag. Microwave on 100% (HIGH) 30 to 45 seconds or just until warm. Arrange pita bread halves around meatball mixture. Invite guests to spoon 2 meatballs with sauce into each pita bread half. Makes 4 servings.

Yogurt Sauce:
Place zucchini in a large microwave-safe bowl. Cover tightly. Microwave on 100% (HIGH) 3 minutes. Drain zucchini and stir in tomatoes, yogurt and mint.

Jamaican Stuffed Pumpkin

Jamaica

Don't wait for Halloween to serve this. Use any of the beautiful round fall and winter squash.

1 small whole pumpkin or Hubbard squash (8- to 10-inches in diameter)

2 lbs. ground beef

6 ozs. ground smoked ham

3 large onions, finely chopped

2 cloves garlic, minced

1 green bell pepper, seeded, finely chopped

2 teaspoons salt

2 teaspoons dried leaf oregano

1 teaspoon black pepper

1/2 teaspoon crushed dried red pepper flakes

1/2 cup dark raisins

1/2 cup chopped pimiento-stuffed green olives

1 (8-oz.) can tomato sauce

3 eggs, beaten

Cut a 5-inch circular lid from top of pumpkin and discard. Remove seeds and membrane. Place pumpkin in a large microwave-safe dish. Cover tightly. Microwave on 100% (HIGH) 10 to 15 minutes or just until tender. Let stand, covered, 10 minutes. In a large microwave-safe bowl, combine ground beef and ham, onions, garlic and bell pepper. Microwave on 100% (HIGH) 5 minutes. Stir to break up beef. Microwave on 100% (HIGH) 4 to 5 minutes more or until beef is no longer pink. Stir in salt, oregano, black pepper, red pepper flakes, raisins, olives and tomato sauce. Microwave on 100% (HIGH) 5 minutes, stirring once during cooking. Quickly stir in beaten eggs. Spoon meat mixture into pumpkin. Cover top with plastic wrap. Microwave on 100% (HIGH) 10 minutes. Let stand, covered, 10 minutes. To serve, scoop out meat mixture and pumpkin. Makes 8 servings.

Meatball Sandwiches

Broodjes — Holland

Hearty sandwiches made with good rolls are a popular Dutch meal. The fillings range from meatballs to liverwurst, and beer is the preferred beverage to serve with them.

- **3/4 lb. ground beef**
- **1/4 lb. ground pork sausage**
- **1/3 cup fresh dark rye bread crumbs**
- **1 tablespoon chopped fresh parsley**
- **2 tablespoons Dijon-style mustard**
- **1 egg**
- **1/2 teaspoon salt**
- **1 (12-oz.) can flat beer**
- **12 small buns, split**
- **12 slices Edam cheese**

In a large bowl, combine ground beef, sausage, bread crumbs, parsley, mustard, egg and salt. Mix well. Shape meat mixture in 12 balls. Place meatballs in a large flat-bottom microwave-safe dish. Cover tightly. Microwave on 100% (HIGH) 3 minutes. Gently turn meatballs upside down, keeping round shape. Re-cover and microwave on 100% (HIGH) 3 to 4 minutes more or until no longer pink in center. Pour beer into dish. Re-cover and microwave on 100% (HIGH) 6 to 8 minutes. Place a hot meatball on bottom of each split bun. Top with a slice of cheese and replace tops of buns. Makes 12 small sandwiches.

Veal Scallops in Marsala

Scaloppini al Marsala — Italy

The word scallop is used to mean a thin slice of veal which some early cook probably felt looked like a sea scallop shell. The French call it escalopes de veau *and the Italians* scallopini.

- **3 tablespoons butter or margarine**
- **1/2 teaspoon ground sage**
- **4 (1/4-inch-thick) veal scallops (about 1 lb.), pounded 1/8-inch thick**
- **1/4 cup Marsala wine**
- **8 ozs. fresh mushrooms, thinly sliced**

Place butter and sage in a large flat-bottom microwave-safe dish. Microwave on 100% (HIGH) 30 seconds or until butter is melted. Mix well. Lay veal flat in seasoned butter. Cover loosely with waxed paper. Microwave on 100% (HIGH) 2 minutes. Turn veal over and re-cover. Microwave on 100% (HIGH) 1 to 3 minutes more or just until veal is no longer pink. Remove veal to a serving platter. Cover to keep warm. Combine wine with liquid in dish. Add mushrooms. Cover tightly. Microwave on 100% (HIGH) 2 to 3 minutes, stirring once during cooking. Spoon mushrooms and sauce over veal. Makes 4 servings.

Shepherd's Pie

England

A top crust of mashed potatoes on ground beef is the classic Shepherd's Pie. To make this a heartier dish, you might want to add some cooked carrots and green beans.

1 lb. lean ground beef
1 large onion, minced
1/3 cup beef broth
1 tablespoon ketchup
1 tablespoon Worcestershire sauce
1 tablespoon Dijon-style mustard
1 teaspoon salt
1/4 teaspoon black pepper
1/3 cup milk
2 tablespoons butter or margarine
3 cups cooked mashed potatoes
Paprika
Fresh parsley sprig to garnish

Crumble beef into an 8-inch flat-bottom round microwave-safe dish. Sprinkle with onions. Cover tightly. Microwave on 100% (HIGH) 4 minutes. Stir in beef broth, ketchup, Worcestershire sauce, mustard, salt and pepper. Microwave on 100% (HIGH) 2 to 3 minutes or until beef is no longer pink. In a 2-cup glass measure, microwave milk and butter on 100% (HIGH) 2 to 2-1/2 minutes or until butter is melted. In a medium-size bowl, stir hot buttered milk into mashed potatoes to make an easy spreading consistency. Smooth top of meat mixture level. Spread with mashed potato mixture, or if desired, pipe mashed potato mixture onto top of pie with a pastry tube fitted with a large plain tube. Cover tightly. Microwave on 100% (HIGH) 4 to 5 minutes or until heated through. Sprinkle with paprika and garnish with parsley. Makes 4 to 6 servings.

Beef Tacos *(Photo on page 111)*

Tacos de Carne — *Mexico*

A favorite that is better than ever with shredded beef.

1-1/2 lbs. lean beef stew meat, cut in 1-inch cubes
2 teaspoons salt
2 cups water
1 to 2 cups dairy sour cream
3/4 cup chopped green onions
1 cup shredded Cheddar or Monterey Jack cheese (4 ozs.)
8 taco shells
1 (7-oz.) can salsa
Guacamole, if desired

In a large flat-bottom microwave-safe glass dish, combine beef, salt and water. Cover tightly. Microwave on 50% (MEDIUM) 35 to 40 minutes or until beef is tender, stirring twice during cooking. Drain well. Shred beef. In a large bowl, mix shredded beef, 1 cup of sour cream, green onions and 3/4 cup of cheese. Spoon beef filling into taco shells. Arrange on a microwave-safe serving plate. Microwave on 50% (MEDIUM) 5 minutes or until hot. Sprinkle with remaining cheese. Spoon salsa over cheese. Top tacos with sour cream, if desired, and serve with guacamole, if desired. Makes 4 servings.

Shepherd's Pie, above.

Ground Lamb Casserole

Pasteetsah *Greece*

Some spell this pastitio *while others spell it* pasteetsah. *Either ground lamb or ground beef can be used. This is a popular Greek casserole that is made in many slightly different variations, depending on which area of Greece the family came from.*

1 medium-size onion, diced
1 clove garlic, minced
1 lb. ground lamb
1/4 teaspoon salt
1/4 teaspoon ground cinnamon
1/2 cup chopped fresh or drained canned tomatoes
3 tablespoons tomato paste
2 tablespoons butter or margarine, softened
2 tablespoons all-purpose flour
1 cup milk
1/2 cup ricotta cheese
1 egg, beaten
6 ozs. spaghetti, cooked, drained
2 ozs. freshly grated Parmesan cheese

In a large microwave-safe bowl, combine onion, garlic, ground lamb, salt and cinnamon. Cover tightly. Microwave on 100% (HIGH) 5 minutes, stirring twice during cooking to break up lamb in small pieces. Stir in tomatoes and tomato paste. To make white sauce, in a medium-size microwave-safe bowl, combine butter and flour. Microwave on 100% (HIGH) 30 to 45 seconds or until butter is melted. Stir well, then mix in milk. Microwave on 100% (HIGH) 3 to 4 minutes or until mixture starts to thicken, stirring twice during cooking. Whisk in ricotta cheese and egg. To assemble, spoon 1/2 of cooked spaghetti into an 8-inch-square microwave-safe dish. Spread lamb mixture on spaghetti. Sprinkle with 1/2 of Parmesan cheese. Spoon remaining spaghetti on Parmesan cheese. Cover with white sauce and remaining Parmesan cheese. Cover tightly. Microwave on 70% (MEDIUM-HIGH) 6 to 8 minutes or until heated through. Makes 6 servings.

East Indian Lamb & Eggplant

Korma — *India*

Ginger is a spice usually associated with oriental cooking. It fits easily into Indian cookery and is often found in curries.

1 lb. boneless lean lamb, diced
1 cup drained canned tomatoes, finely chopped
1 (6-oz.) can tomato paste
1/2 teaspoon ground ginger
1/4 teaspoon ground cinnamon
5 green onions, chopped
3 tablespoons finely chopped fresh parsley
1 teaspoon salt
1/4 teaspoon black pepper
4 (1-inch-thick) slices eggplant
1/4 cup butter, melted
1/2 cup plain yogurt

In a 2-quart microwave-safe dish, combine lamb, tomatoes, tomato paste, ginger, cinnamon, green onions, parsley, salt and pepper. Cover with waxed paper. Microwave on 100% (HIGH) 8 to 9 minutes, stirring twice during cooking. Stir well. Re-cover with waxed paper. Microwave on 50% (MEDIUM) 20 to 25 minutes or until lamb is tender. Brush both sides of eggplant with butter. Arrange on a microwave-safe serving platter. Cover tightly. Microwave on 100% (HIGH) 5 minutes. To serve, spoon lamb mixture over eggplant slices. Top with spoonfuls of yogurt. Makes 4 servings.

Leg of Lamb

Gigot D'Agneau — *France*

Lamb, like beef, takes about seven minutes per pound to cook in the microwave oven. The French, as many Americans do, prefer lamb slightly rare in the center. The majority of English people prefer their "Joint of Lamb" well done. Whatever degree of doneness you prefer, an instant-read special microwave meat thermometer is the most accurate way to cook a leg of lamb exactly as you like it.

1 (3 lb.) leg of lamb
3 cloves garlic, thinly sliced

Make small slits in lamb. Push in garlic slices. Place lamb in a microwave-safe roasting pan, fat side down. Microwave on 100% (HIGH) 10 minutes. Turn lamb over. Microwave on 100% (HIGH) 11 to 15 minutes more. Microwave lamb to 120F (50C) for rare, 140F (60C) for medium or 150F (65C) for well done. Cover with foil. Let stand 10 minutes and cut in slices. Makes 5 to 8 servings.

Irish Stew

I r e l a n d

A cool climate combined with abundant lamb and hearty vegetables made the staple Irish Stew popular in Ireland. It is now enjoyed in many countries.

1-1/2 lbs. boneless lean lamb, cut in 1-1/2-inch cubes

2 tablespoons butter or margarine

2 medium-size onions, chopped

1 cup water

2 cups carrots, thinly sliced

3 medium-size potatoes, peeled, cut in chunks

1/2 head green cabbage, cut in 4 wedges

Place lamb, butter and onions in a 3-quart microwave-safe dish. Cover tightly. Microwave on 100% (HIGH) 10 to 12 minutes or until lamb is brown, stirring twice during cooking. Add water, carrots and potatoes. Re-cover and microwave on 50% (MEDIUM) 30 to 40 minutes or until meat is tender. Add cabbage. Re-cover and microwave on 100% (HIGH) 5 to 7 minutes or until cabbage is tender. Makes 4 to 6 servings.

Fettuccine with Prosciutto

Fettuccine e Prosciutto

I t a l y

Parmesan cheese is a hard cheese originally made in Italy in the 1200's. If you can get a good aged Italian Parmesan, be sure to use it. American pregrated Parmesan cheese will do, but it is much milder in flavor.

4 ozs. proscuitto ham, diced

2 medium-size tomatoes, seeded, diced

1/2 cup fresh or frozen green peas

1/4 cup butter or margarine

1 cup whipping cream

1/2 cup grated Parmesan cheese

8 ozs. fettuccine, cooked, drained

In a large microwave-safe bowl, combine ham, tomatoes and green peas. Cover tightly. Microwave on 100% (HIGH) 2-1/2 to 3 minutes or until ham is sizzling. Add butter and cream. Microwave on 100% (HIGH) 3 minutes or until butter is melted. Stir in Parmesan cheese. Add hot fettuccine and toss quickly. Makes 2 to 4 servings.

Lamb & Bulgar Pie

Kibbee — *Middle East*

Bulgar is a grain often used in Middle Eastern cookery. It is available in speciality stores or in the ethnic sections of larger supermarkets.

1/3 cup bulgar
1 lb. ground lamb
1/4 cup minced onion
1/8 teaspoon dried leaf oregano
1-1/2 teaspoons salt
Black pepper to taste
2 tablespoons butter or margarine

Nut Stuffing:
1/2 cup ground lamb
1/3 cup pine nuts
1/8 teaspoon salt
1 tablespoon butter or margarine
Black pepper to taste

Prepare Nut Stuffing. In a large bowl, cover bulgar with water. Let stand 30 minutes, then drain well. Mix bulgar with ground lamb, onion, oregano and salt. Season with pepper. Mix well. Pat 1/2 of bulgar mixture into a 9-inch glass pie plate. Top with Nut Stuffing, then pat rest of bulgar mixture over stuffing. Cut in 8 wedges. (It is difficult to cut after microwaving.) Dot with butter. Place in microwave oven on an inverted microwave-safe saucer. Microwave on 100% (HIGH) 6 minutes. Rotate dish one-half turn. Microwave on 70% (MEDIUM-HIGH) 8 to 10 minutes more. Makes 4 to 8 servings.

Nut Stuffing:
Crumble ground lamb into a medium-size microwave-safe bowl. Mix in pine nuts, salt and butter. Season with pepper. Mix well. Microwave on 100% (HIGH) 2 minutes. Stir to break up lamb. Microwave on 100% (HIGH) 2 to 3 minutes more or until lamb is no longer pink.

Frankfurters à la Reuben

U. S. A.

While the ingredients in this sandwich have Germanic overtones, this is truly an American combination.

8 frankfurters
4 slices pumpernickel bread, toasted
1 (8-oz.) can sauerkraut, drained
1/4 cup Thousand Island dressing
1/2 cup shredded Swiss cheese (2 ozs.)

Using a sharp knife, make cuts into frankfurters 1/2-inch apart and almost through. Place toast on a microwave-safe plate. Top each slice of toast with 3 tablespoons of sauerkraut, 1 tablespoon of dressing and 2 frankfurters. Microwave on 100% (HIGH) 4 minutes, rotating plate one-fourth turn after 2 minutes. Sprinkle cheese over frankfurters. Microwave on 100% (HIGH) 1 minute or until cheese is melted. Makes 4 servings.

Sauteed Pork & Onion

Mucklica — *Y u g o s l a v i a*

Pork and onions with a touch of peppers is a common combination found in the Balkan countries. With their ever changing boundries, it's hard to assign this dish to a certain country.

4 medium-size onions, thinly sliced
2 tablespoons vegetable oil
1 teaspoon salt
1 teaspoon sweet paprika
1/2 teaspoon black pepper
1/4 teaspoon dried red chili pepper
2 (1-lb.) pork tenderloins, cut in 1-inch cubes
1 red bell pepper, seeded, sliced
2 ozs. feta cheese, crumbled

In a large flat-bottom microwave-safe dish, combine onions, oil, salt, paprika, black pepper and red chili pepper. Cover loosely with waxed paper. Microwave on 100% (HIGH) 5 minutes. Stir. Microwave on 100% (HIGH) 3 to 4 minutes more or until onions are tender. Stir in cubed pork. Cover tightly. Microwave on 100% (HIGH) 4 to 5 minutes. Stir. Microwave on 100% (HIGH) 4 to 5 minutes more or until pork is no longer pink in center. Stir in bell pepper. Microwave on 100% (HIGH) 2 minutes. Sprinkle with feta cheese. Makes 6 servings.

Barbecue Country-Style Ribs

U. S. A.

Use lower power levels to make pork more tender when cooking in the microwave oven. Slow cooking at 50% (MEDIUM) results in tender ribs that melt in your mouth. By rearranging the ribs several times during microwaving, the ribs will cook more evenly. Use hot pads when handling the cooking bag and dish.

3 to 3-1/2 lbs. country-style pork ribs, cut in serving-size pieces
1 cup water
1-1/2 cups chili sauce
1/2 cup orange marmalade
1/3 cup red wine vinegar
1 tablespoon Worcestershire sauce
1/2 teaspoon celery seed

Place ribs in an 14'' x 20'' oven cooking bag. Set in a large microwave-safe dish. Pour water over ribs. Tie bag loosely and pierce bag several times with tip of a sharp knife. Microwave on 50% (MEDIUM) 20 minutes. Turn ribs over and rearrange in bag. Microwave on 50% (MEDIUM) 20 minutes more. Meanwhile, to prepare sauce, in a small bowl, combine chili sauce, marmalade, vinegar, Worcestershire sauce and celery seed. Remove ribs from cooking bag and place in large flat-bottom microwave-safe dish. Pour sauce over ribs, turning to coat completely. Cover tightly. Microwave on 50% (MEDIUM) 15 to 20 minutes or until ribs are tender, rearranging ribs after 8 to 10 minutes. Makes 4 to 5 servings.

Beef Tacos, page 104.

Hot & Spicy Pork Chili

U. S. A.

If you prefer a spicier chili, consider using hot pork sausage. Hot & Spicy Pork Chili is just as good the second time around! When reheating leftovers in the microwave oven, cover the leftovers and microwave at a power level lower than what was used to microwave the food originally. This ensures even heating.

1 lb. boneless pork shoulder, cut in 1/2-inch pieces

1 lb. bulk pork sausage

1/2 cup chopped green bell pepper

1/2 onion, chopped

2 cloves garlic, minced

1 (28-oz.) can tomatoes, coarsely chopped, juice reserved

1 (15-1/4-oz.) can kidney beans, drained

1 (8-oz.) can tomato sauce

3/4 cup flat beer

1-1/2 tablespoons chili powder

1/2 teaspoon salt

1/2 teaspoon ground cumin

1/8 teaspoon crushed red pepper flakes, if desired

Dairy sour cream, if desired

Shredded cheddar cheese, if desired

In a 3-quart microwave-safe dish, combine pork, sausage, bell pepper, onion and garlic. Cover tightly. Microwave on 50% (MEDIUM) 15 minutes, stirring every 5 minutes. Stir in tomatoes with reserved juice, kidney beans, tomato sauce, beer, chili powder, salt, cumin and red pepper flakes, if desired. Re-cover and microwave on 100% (HIGH) 20 minutes. Stir well. Microwave on 50% (MEDIUM) 30 minutes. Stir and remove cover. Microwave on 50% (MEDIUM) 20 minutes more. Garnish with sour cream and shredded cheddar cheese, if desired. Makes 6 servings.

Pork Stuffed Cucumber

Rong Hwong Gwa China

Cucumbers in the U.S.A. are usually considered a salad vegetable. When cooked and filled, a new deminsion is added.

2 medium-size cucumbers, peeled
1/2 lb. ground pork
1/2 teaspoon minced gingerroot
6 water chestnuts, finely chopped
2 tablespoons soy sauce
2 tablespoons sliced green onion
1 tablespoon chopped fresh cilantro

Slice cucumbers lengthwise, scoop out seeds. Break up ground pork in a medium-size microwave-safe bowl. Combine pork with ginger, water chestnuts, soy sauce, green onion and cilantro. Microwave on 100% (HIGH) 2 minutes. Stir and break up pork in very small pieces. Microwave on 100% (HIGH) 2 to 3 minutes more or until pork is no longer pink. Spoon pork mixture into cucumber cavities. Place filled cucumbers on a microwave-safe serving platter. Cover tightly. Microwave on 100% (HIGH) 4 to 5 minutes or until cucumber is tender. Makes 4 to 6 servings.

Ginger Pork

Shoga Agemono Japan

Stir-frying is a very quick cooking technique. Cooking in the microwave can give similar, very good results.

2 (3-inch-long) pieces gingerroot, peeled, cut in very fine julienne strips
2 tablespoons vegetable oil
3/4 lb. pork tenderloin, cut in 1/8-inch-thick slices
1/2 lb. small bay scallops
1/2 lb. small fresh mushrooms
1 lb. fresh asparagus or 1 (10-oz.) pkg. frozen asparagus, cut in 2-inch lengths
3 tablespoons soy sauce
2 tablespoons dry sherry
1 tablespoon cornstarch
1/2 teaspoon sugar

In a medium-size flat-bottom microwave-safe glass dish, combine gingerroot and oil. Microwave on 100% (HIGH) 2 to 2-1/2 minutes; do not burn. Remove and reserve gingerroot. Place pork in remaining oil in dish. Cover tightly. Microwave on 100% (HIGH) 2 minutes. Stir well. Microwave on 100% (HIGH) 2 to 3 minutes more or until pork is no longer pink. Mix in scallops, mushrooms and asparagus. Cover tightly. Microwave on 100% (HIGH) 3 to 3-1/2 minutes more or until scallops are opaque. In a small bowl, mix soy sauce, sherry, cornstarch and sugar. Pour over pork mixture. Microwave on 100% (HIGH) 1 minute. Spoon mixture into a serving dish. Sprinkle with reserved gingerroot. Makes 4 to 5 servings.

Tangy Marinated Pork Chops

U. S. A.

To make marinating easy, place the pork chops in a plastic bag and set in a baking dish. Pour the marinade over the chops and close the bag.

3 tablespoons bottled steak sauce
2 tablespoons vegetable oil
1 tablespoon red wine vinegar
1 teaspoon dark-brown sugar
1 teaspoon Worcestershire sauce
4 (6-oz.) boneless pork top loin chops, 1-inch thick

To prepare marinade, in a small bowl, combine steak sauce, oil, vinegar, brown sugar and Worcestershire sauce. Place chops in a plastic bag. Pour marinade over chops, turning to coat chops completely. Tie bag securely and refrigerate 1 to 2 hours, turning chops over after 1 hour. Drain marinade into a 1-cup glass measure. Place chops in a medium-size flat-bottom microwave-safe dish. Cover tightly. Microwave on 30% (MEDIUM LOW) 9 minutes. Turn chops over. Rotate dish one-half turn. Re-cover and microwave on 30% (MEDIUM LOW) 9 minutes more. Microwave marinade on 100% (HIGH) 1 minute. Pour marinade over pork chops. Makes 4 servings.

Apples & Sausage

C a n a d a

Pure maple syrup is indeed a treat! It takes something like forty gallons of sap to produce one gallon of syrup. Maple trees can be found all along the eastern part of the North American Continent—Quebec, Canada is as well known for its maple syrup as is our state of Vermont.

1-1/2 lbs. pork dinner sausages (large German-type)
1 cup maple syrup
1/2 cup distilled white vinegar
5 medium-size cooking apples, cored, cut in 1/2-inch slices

Pierce sausages 3 or 4 times with a fork. Place sausages in a medium-size flat-bottom microwave-safe dish. Cover loosely with waxed paper. Microwave on 100% (HIGH) 4 minutes. Turn sausages over. Re-cover and microwave on 100% (HIGH) 3 to 4 minutes more or until no longer pink in center. Remove sausages and keep warm. Combine syrup and vinegar in dish. Spread apples in dish. Cover tightly. Microwave on 100% (HIGH) 4 minutes. Turn apples over. Re-cover and microwave on 100% (HIGH) 2 to 3 minutes more or until apples are tender. Stir sausages back into syrup mixture. Makes 4 servings.

Jambalaya

Southern U. S. A.

Creole cookery runs a wide gamut of dishes and seasonings, from dark, earthy stews to clear seafood stocks. But probably the best known Creole dishes are the flavorful tomato-base red sauces found on menus around the world. In these dishes can be found the meshing of the many influences which shaped the distinctive Creole cruisine—French, Spanish, African and American Indian.

1 lb. mild Italian sausage
1/2 cup chopped onion
1/2 cup chopped green bell pepper
1/2 cup sliced celery
1 clove garlic, crushed
1 (8-oz.) can tomato sauce
3 cups water
1 cup cubed cooked ham
3/4 cup uncooked white long-grain rice
1/2 teaspoon dried thyme leaves, crushed
1/4 teaspoon chili powder
1/8 teaspoon black pepper
1 bay leaf

Remove casings from sausage. Break up sausage into a 10-inch microwave-safe dish. Mix in onion, bell pepper, celery and garlic. Microwave on 100% (HIGH) 5 to 7 minutes or until sausage is no longer pink and onion is translucent. Drain excess fat. Stir in tomato sauce, water, ham, rice, thyme, chili powder and pepper. Add bay leaf. Cover tightly. Microwave on 50% (MEDIUM) 20 minutes. Stir. Re-cover and microwave on 50% (MEDIUM) 8 to 10 minutes more or until rice is tender. Remove and discard bay leaf. Makes 4 servings.

Honey Mustard Steaks

U. S. A.

Steak is considered a special occasion food and is usually barbecued or broiled. This dish is special enough to be served anytime. Preparing it in the microwave oven means the clean-up is extra easy.

3 medium-size carrots, cut in 1/4-inch rounds

2 medium-size zucchini, cut in 1/4-inch rounds

1 medium-size onion, cut in 1/4-inch rounds

2 tablespoons butter or margarine

4 (4-oz.) boneless top sirloin steaks

1 cup beef bouillon

1 tablespoon cornstarch

1/4 cup dry sherry

1 tablespoon Dijon-style mustard

2 tablespoons honey

In a medium-size microwave-safe shallow casserole dish, combine carrots, zucchini and onion. Dot with butter. Cover tightly. Microwave on 100% (HIGH) 5 minutes. Let stand 10 minutes. Place steaks on a microwave-safe serving platter. Cover loosely. Microwave on 70% (MEDIUM-HIGH) 4 to 5 minutes for medium-rare steaks, turning over after 3 minutes. To prepare sauce, pour meat juice into a 2-cup glass measure. Whisk in bouillon, cornstarch, sherry, mustard and honey. Microwave on 100% (HIGH) 3 to 5 minutes or until mixture comes to a boil and thickens slightly. Drain vegetables and stir sauce into drained vegetables. Spoon over steaks. Makes 4 servings.

Side Dishes

Vegetables have historically been the mainstay of the masses. When the pilgrims landed in New England, they subsisted on the native crops, corn, squash and beans, they found growing there. The potato famine in Ireland in the 1800's caused masses of people to leave, searching for food.

The eggplant, while internationally an important vegetable, has not found much importance in American cooking. It originated in India where it is still widely used. It then traveled to French kitchens where it was called *aubergine* for its beautiful purple color. Louis XIV liked it so well he grew it in his gardens at Versaille. The English call it *aubergine* too. Perhaps if when it reached America the name was different, it would have been more popular.

Nothing is more distasteful to a Chinese cook than overcooked vegetables. Vegetables are considered done just as soon as they are tender, but are still crisp and bright in color. I think it is due to the Chinese tender-crisp method of cooking and the microwave oven that in America our preferences have finally shifted away from overcooked, mushy, colorless vegetables.

In France very fresh colorful vegetables are often served as a course by themselves to show their importance in the meal. One or more types will be served hot with a sauce over the top.

Vegetables sauteed in olive oil or batter dipped and fried are often served as a first course in Spain. An aromatic tomato sauce may bind vegetables with sausages or aged ham to create a hearty one-dish meal. Fried potatoes often accompany a meat dish to round out the meal.

Rice and grain dishes are another universal food. Rice found its way from China, where it is a major part of the Chinese diet, to Italy with its famous *risottos*, and to Mexico where again it is a hearty basis for many meals. *Pilaf* is a grain-based dish made from combinations of rice, pasta and bulgar. The bulgar-based *pilaf* originated in the Middle East. The Greek version is called *pilafi,* in Turkey it's *pilav* and *pullao* in India. To make *pilaf* the grain is first sauteed, then liquid and seasonings are added as it cooks. It is a very economical dish which is probably why it has remained popular. Similar rice based dishes are found in China as fried rice, Spain has its *paella* and in the Southern United States we have jambalaya.

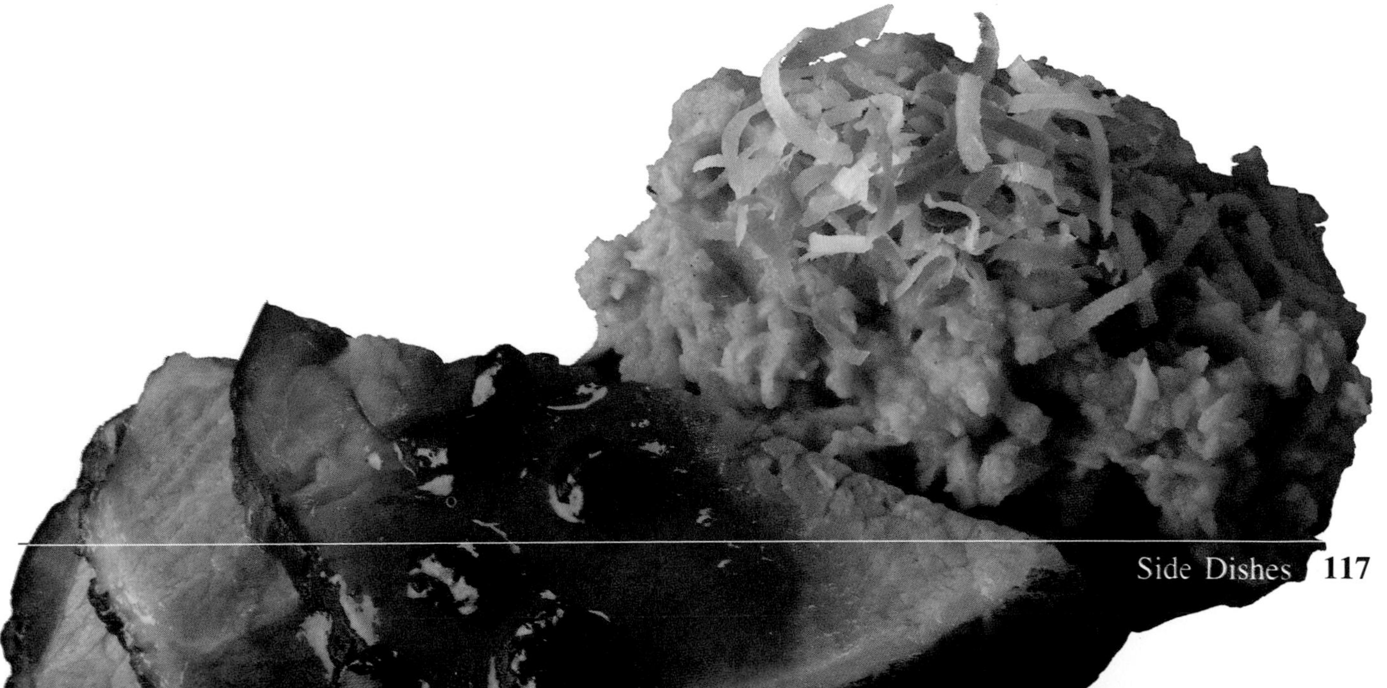

Cauliflower & Mushrooms

Chop Choy — China

Cauliflower is not often thought of as a typical oriental vegetable, but it appears quite often in oriental dishes.

1 small head cauliflower, cut in bite-size flowerettes
10 medium-size fresh mushrooms, thinly sliced
1/4 cup water chestnuts, thinly sliced
3/4 cup chicken broth
2 tablespoons soy sauce
1 tablespoon cornstarch

Place cauliflower in a medium-size deep microwave-safe casserole dish. Cover tightly. Microwave on 100% (HIGH) 4 to 5 minutes or until tender. Add mushrooms and water chestnuts. In a small bowl, combine chicken broth, soy sauce and cornstarch, stirring well to dissolve cornstarch. Pour over cauliflower mixture. Re-cover and microwave on 100% (HIGH) 2 to 3 minutes, stirring 2 to 3 times to coat cauliflower. Makes 4 to 6 servings.

Lima Beans in Tomato Sauce

Frijoles Verdes con Salsa — Spain

This tomato sauce is made from fresh tomatoes sauteed in olive oil until the tomatoes are very soft and resemble a sauce in texture. Green beans would be a good substitution for the lima beans.

2 tablespoons olive oil
2 medium-size tomatoes, peeled, seeded, finely chopped
1 medium-size onion, finely chopped
1/2 clove garlic, minced
2 (10-oz.) pkgs. frozen lima beans

In a medium-size microwave-safe casserole dish, combine olive oil and tomatoes. Cover tightly. Microwave on 100% (HIGH) 6 to 7 minutes or until tomatoes are very soft. Add onion and garlic. Re-cover and microwave on 100% (HIGH) 2 to 3 minutes or until onion is tender. Stir in lima beans. Re-cover and microwave on 100% (HIGH) 8 to 10 minutes or until beans are tender. Makes 4 to 6 servings.

Little Peas

Petits Pois — France

Peas steamed with lettuce leaves is a common combination in France, but in the U.S. we generally reserve lettuce only for salads. If you have fresh peas by all means use them, if not substitute frozen petite peas.

4 large iceberg lettuce leaves

3 lbs. small fresh green peas, shelled, or 2 (10-oz.) pkgs. frozen petite green peas, thawed

1/2 teaspoon sugar

1 tablespoon butter or margarine

Line a medium-size microwave-safe serving bowl with 3 lettuce leaves. Add peas, sprinkle with sugar and dot with butter. Top with remaining lettuce leaf. Cover tightly. Microwave on 100% (HIGH) 4 to 5 minutes or just until peas are tender. Makes 4 to 6 servings.

Tomatoes Provence Style

Pommes Provencale — France

To make great fresh bread crumbs, process one-half of a slice of white bread, crust removed, in a blender or food processor until coarsely chopped.

2 tablespoons olive oil

1/4 teaspoon salt

1 clove garlic, minced

1/2 teaspoon dried leaf oregano

Freshly ground black pepper to taste

4 large tomatoes, cut in half crosswise, seeded

1 tablespoon finely chopped fresh parsley

2 tablespoons coarsely chopped bread crumbs

In a large flat bottom microwave-safe casserole dish, combine olive oil, salt, garlic and oregano. Season with pepper. Place tomatoes in dish, cut side down. Cover tightly. Microwave on 100% (HIGH) 3 minutes. Brush tomatoes to coat with oil. Re-cover and microwave on 100% (HIGH) 2 to 3 minutes more or until tomatoes are tender. Place tomatoes on serving platter. Stir parsley and bread crumbs into seasoned oil in dish. Microwave on 100% (HIGH) 2 minutes. Spoon crumb mixture over tomatoes. Makes 4 servings.

Coconut Sweet Potatoes

U. S. A. — Hawaii

The coconut is steeped in hot milk to extract flavor. Try this for a change with your holiday turkey for a memorable meal.

1/2 cup sweetened flaked coconut
1/2 cup milk
1 (16-oz.) can sweet potatoes, drained
1/8 teaspoon ground ginger
1/4 teaspoon ground cinnamon
2 tablespoons butter or margarine, softened
1/4 cup drained crushed pineapple

In a small bowl, combine coconut and milk. Microwave on 100% (HIGH) 2 minutes or just until milk is hot. Let stand 10 minutes. In a large bowl, mash sweet potatoes with ginger, cinnamon and butter. Drain milk and reserve coconut. Add hot coconut milk to sweet potatoes and mix until smooth. Reserve 2 tablespoons of coconut. Stir remaining coconut and pineapple into sweet potato mixture. Spoon into a medium-size microwave-safe serving dish. Cover tightly. Microwave on 100% (HIGH) 5 to 6 minutes or until hot. Toast reserved coconut and sprinkle over sweet potatoes. Makes 4 servings.

Duchesse Potatoes

U. S. A.

Duchesse potatoes are mashed potatoes that are piped onto a serving platter or plate for decoration. I find the microwave is perfect for preparing this dish because the potatoes are usually broiled to reheat them after piping. By reheating the potatoes with the microwave oven, they do not dry out.

4 medium-size sweet potatoes or baking potatoes
1/2 cup butter or margarine
2 eggs
1/8 teaspoon ground nutmeg
1/2 cup milk

Using a fork, prick skins of potatoes. Microwave on 100% (HIGH) 6 minutes. Turn potatoes over. Microwave on 100% (HIGH) 7 to 8 minutes more or until tender. Wrap potatoes individually in foil or let stand in microwave with door shut 10 minutes. Peel potatoes. In a large bowl, mash potatoes by hand or with an electric mixer. Stir in butter, eggs, nutmeg and enough milk to make mixture thin enough to pipe. Using a pastry bag fitted with a large star tip, pipe potatoes in rosettes or a ring around a microwave-safe platter or plate. If desired, prepare ahead and refrigerate until ready to serve. To heat potatoes, microwave platter on 100% (HIGH) 30 to 60 seconds or until heated. Makes 4 to 6 servings.

Clockwise from top left: Fresh green beans; Coconut Sweet Potatoes, above; Baked ham with Cumberland Sauce, page 56.

Vermont Sweet Potatoes

U. S. A.

Vermont is famous for its maple syrup, although it's rare that you find real maple in most syrups now. Fresh sweet potatoes can be easily cooked in the microwave oven, but I find using canned sweet potatoes even easier!

1 large red cooking apple, cored, cut in 1/2-inch wedges

1/4 cup butter or margarine

1/4 cup maple syrup

1 (24-oz.) can sweet potatoes, undrained

Place apple and butter in a medium-size flat bottom microwave-safe casserole dish. Cover tightly. Microwave on 100% (HIGH) 3 minutes. Stir in maple syrup and sweet potatoes. Re-cover and microwave on 100% (HIGH) 5 minutes. Makes 4 to 6 servings.

Potatoes Anna

Pommes Anna *France*

The precise design of the potato slices make this dish special. I have added a little paprika to give the potatoes more color definition. It can be left out if you prefer. Use a good baking potato as it will hold its shape better.

1/2 cup butter or margarine

1/2 teaspoon paprika

2 lbs. baking potatoes, peeled, thinly sliced

1 teaspoon salt

Freshly ground black pepper to taste

Place 1/4 cup of butter and paprika in an 8-inch round microwave-safe cake dish. Microwave on 100% (HIGH) 1 minute or until butter melts. Swirl melted butter to completely coat dish. Layer 1/3 of potato slicee in a circular fashion on sides and bottom of dish. Dot with 2 tablespoons of butter. Sprinkle with salt. Season with pepper. Repeat procedure twice with remaining ingredients. Cover tightly. Microwave on 100% (HIGH) 8 to 10 minutes or until potatoes in center are tender. Let stand, covered, 5 minutes. To serve, invert on a serving dish. Makes 4 to 6 servings.

Potatoes with Gruyére Cheese

Pommes au Fromage *France*

If you're serving this with a chicken dish, substitue chicken broth in place of the beef broth.

4 medium-size baking poatoes, peeled, thinly sliced
1 teaspoon salt
1/4 teaspoon black pepper
1/4 teaspoon ground nutmeg
1-1/2 cups shredded Gruyére or Swiss cheese (5 ozs.)
1/3 cup beef broth

Arrange potatoes in 3 layers in a medium-size flat bottom microwave-safe casserole dish, sprinkling each layer with salt, pepper, nutmeg and cheese. Pour broth over top layer. Cover tightly. Microwave on 100% (HIGH) 8 to 10 minutes or until potatoes are tender. Let stand 5 minutes before serving. Makes 4 to 6 servings.

Two Cabbages in Wine

Zweifarben Kraut im Wein *Germany*

The word for cabbage in German is kohl, *but shredded cabbage is called* kraut. *Pickled cabbage is called* sauerkraut, *which is a familar word to us all.*

3 slices bacon
1 medium-size onion, chopped
2 medium-size apples, peeled, cored, chopped
1/2 small red cabbage, thinly sliced
1/2 small green cabbage, thinly sliced
1/2 cup dry white wine
1 tablespoon sugar
1 tablespoon cider vinegar
Salt and black pepper to taste

Place bacon in a large deep microwave-safe casserole dish. Cover with a paper towel. Microwave on 100% (HIGH) 3 to 4 minutes or until crisp. Drain bacon on a paper towel, crumble and set aside. Add onion to bacon fat. Microwave on 100% (HIGH) 2 to 2-1/2 minutes or until tender. Stir in apples. Microwave on 100% (HIGH) 1 minute and 30 seconds. Stir in red and green cabbage, wine, sugar and vinegar. Cover tightly. Microwave on 100% (HIGH) 5 minutes. Stir. Re-cover and microwave on 100% (HIGH) 1 to 2 minutes more or just until cabbage is tender. Season with salt and pepper. Makes 4 to 6 servings.

Green Beans with Tomato Sauce

Fagiolini Alla Marinara — *Italy*

Marinara *in Italian means sailor! Use this flavorful tomato sauce on pasta or just warm it and serve with chunks of Italian bread as dippers.*

1 lb. fresh green beans, cut in 2-inch lengths

Marinara Sauce:

1/4 cup olive oil
1 clove garlic, minced
1/2 medium-size onion, chopped
1/4 cup chopped carrot
2 tablespoons chopped fresh parsley
1 (16-oz.) can tomatoes, drained
1 teaspoon dried leaf oregano
1/2 teaspoon dried leaf basil
3 anchovy fillets, if desired

Prepare Marinara Sauce. Place green beans in a medium-size microwave-safe bowl. Cover tightly. Microwave on 100% (HIGH) 3 minutes. Stir. Re-cover and microwave on 100% (HIGH) 2 to 3 minutes more or just until tender. Let stand, covered, 5 minutes. To serve, ladle Marinara Sauce on green beans. Makes 4 servings.

Marinara Sauce:
In a food processor fitted with a metal blade or a blender, process all ingredients to a puree. Pour into a medium-size microwave-safe bowl. Cover tightly. Microwave on 100% (HIGH) 5 minutes. Stir. Microwave on 100% (HIGH) 3 to 5 minutes more or until mixture boils 2 minutes.

Minted Zucchini

Mücver — *Turkey*

If you are a devotee of Turkish cuisine, you would expect this recipe to have fried zucchini. I find that with my method you get the same flavors and a more colorful dish.

3 medium-size zucchini, thinly sliced in rounds
1/4 cup fresh chopped dill weed
2 tablespoons chopped fresh mint leaves
1 tablespoon chopped fresh parsley
2-ozs. feta cheese, crumbled

In a medium-size microwave-safe serving dish, combine zucchini, dill weed and mint. Cover tightly. Microwave on 100% (HIGH) 3 to 5 minutes or just until zucchini are tender. Sprinkle with parsley and feta cheese. Makes 4 servings.

Swiss Chard

U. S. A.

Swiss chard is a dark green leafy vegetable similar to spinach. If it is not available, you can substitute spinach.

3 tablespoons pine nuts
3 tablespoons olive oil
1 clove garlic, minced
1-1/2 lbs. Swiss chard
Salt and black pepper to taste

In a large microwave-safe bowl, combine pine nuts, olive oil and garlic. Microwave on 100% (HIGH) 2 minutes or until nuts are toasted. Add Swiss chard. Cover tightly. Microwave on 100% (HIGH) 3 minutes. Toss Swiss chard to coat with oil. Re-cover and microwave on 100% (HIGH) 1 to 2 minutes more or until Swiss chard is tender. Season with salt and pepper. Makes 4 servings.

Pepper Combination

Peperonata *Italy*

This is a colorful, tasty vegetable combination. Serve it warm or at room temperature.

2 medium-size onions, sliced
2 tablespoons olive oil
1 green bell pepper, thinly sliced lengthwise
1 red bell pepper, thinly sliced lengthwise
1 yellow bell pepper, thinly sliced lengthwise
3 large tomatoes, cut in eighths

In a large microwave-safe bowl, combine onions and oil. Cover tightly. Microwave on 100% (HIGH) 4 to 5 minutes or until onions are tender. Mix in green, red and yellow bell peppers. Re-cover and microwave on 100% (HIGH) 5 to 6 minutes. Stir in tomatoes. Re-cover and microwave on 100% (HIGH) 3 to 4 minutes or until heated through. Makes 4 to 6 servings.

Mushrooms with Hat

Mushrooms Sous Cloche — *France*

Whole fresh mushrooms served under glass are a fancy, light meal. Use a glass cheese dome to top each ramkin or cover tightly with plastic wrap and remove before serving so as not to ruin the effect.

1-1/2 lbs. medium-size fresh mushrooms
1/4 cup butter or margarine
2 teaspoons finely chopped fresh parsley
2 teaspoons fresh lemon juice
1/4 teaspoon dried leaf chervil
Dash of black pepper
1/2 cup whipping cream
2 tablespoons dry sherry
Buttered toast points, if desired, sprinkled with paprika
Fresh herbs and red bell pepper slices to garnish

Place mushrooms, butter, parsley, lemon juice, chervil, pepper and whipping cream in a large microwave-safe bowl. Cover tightly. Microwave on 100% (HIGH) 3 to 5 minutes or until mushrooms are tender. Spoon cooked mushrooms on a plate. Sprinkle with sherry. Cover with a glass dome, if available, or cover tightly with plastic wrap. Microwave on 100% (HIGH) 3 to 4 minutes. Serve with glass dome or remove plastic wrap before serving. If desired, serve with toast points. Garnish with fresh herbs and bell peper slices. Makes 4 servings.

California Carrots

U. S. A.

Carrots and orange flavoring are a tasty combination. The celery seeds add a nutty flavor.

3/4 lb. carrots, peeled, thinly sliced
2 tablespoons butter or margarine
1 teaspoon sugar
1/2 teaspoon celery seeds
1/4 cup orange juice
1/2 teaspoon freshly grated orange peel

Combine all ingredients in a medium-size microwave-safe bowl. Cover tightly. Cook on High (100% power) for 4 minutes. Stir. Cook 1 to 2 minutes longer until tender. Let stand for 5 minutes before uncovering. Makes 4 servings.

Mushrooms with Hat, above.

Carrots Vichy

Carottes Vichy — *France*

Vichy is a town in France where the famous Vichy water is obtained. A small amount of water is used to flavor the carrots. If Vichy water is not available, substitute club soda.

1/2 lb. carrots, cut in 3-inch julienne strips

1/4 cup Vichy water or club soda

Place carrots in a medium-size microwave-safe serving bowl. Add Vichy water. Cover tightly. Microwave on 100% (HIGH) 3 to 5 minutes or until tender. Let stand, covered, 5 minutes. Makes 4 servings.

Zucchini Parmesan

Zucchine al Parmigiano — *Italy*

The authentic Parmigiano Reggiano *has an exotic flavor that makes even the simpliest dish one to remember. It can be found in many specialty cheese shops or delis. If you can't find it, use any Parmesan cheese available.*

3 medium-size zucchini (about 1 lb.), shredded

2 tablespoons butter or margarine

1/4 cup freshly grated Parmesan cheese

Place zucchini in a medium-size microwave-safe casserole dish. Dot with butter. Cover tightly. Microwave on 100% (HIGH) 2 to 3 minutes or until zucchini are tender. Sprinkle with Parmesan cheese. Re-cover and let stand 5 minutes before serving. Makes 4 servings.

Cooking Tip:
To add a fresh taste when cooking whole artichokes, tuck a few slices of lemons in the leaves.

Sauteed Brussels Sprouts

Chow Choy Lui — *China*

I recommend cutting the Brussels sprouts in half lengthwise for a more attractive appearance, plus they will be more flavorful. Fresh Brussels sprouts taste best, but frozen ones will work nicely.

1 clove garlic, minced
2 tablespoons vegetable oil
1 lb. Brussels sprouts, trimmed, cut in half lengthwise
1/2 medium-size red bell pepper, thinly sliced
1 cup chicken stock
2 tablespoons cornstarch
3 tablespoons soy sauce
1 tablespoon dry sherry

Place garlic and oil in flat bottom microwave-safe casserole dish. Microwave on 100% (HIGH) 1 minute. Stir in Brussels sprouts and bell pepper. Cover tightly. Microwave on 100% (HIGH) 3 to 5 minutes or until Brussels sprouts are tender. In a small bowl, combine chicken stock, cornstarch, soy sauce and sherry, stirring well to dissolve cornstarch. Pour over Brussels sprouts. Re-cover and microwave on 100% (HIGH) 2 to 3 minutes or until mixture becomes clear and starts to thicken. Makes 4 servings.

Cabbage with Cheese Sauce

Choux Au Gratin — *France*

I grew up hearing the term pâte a choux *for cream puff pastry. I had to laugh when I realized the word* choux *means cabbage and the French feel cream puffs look like cabbages.*

1 small head green cabbage
2 tablespoons butter or margarine
2 tablespoons all-purpose flour
1 cup milk
1/2 cup grated Gruyére cheese
1/4 teaspoon salt
1/8 teaspoon black pepper
1/4 teaspoon dry mustard
Pinch of nutmeg

Remove core of cabbage and slice very thinly. Place in a medium-size microwave-safe bowl. Cover tightly. Microwave on 100% (HIGH) 4 to 5 minutes or just until limp. Let stand, covered, 5 minutes. To prepare sauce, in a 2-cup glass measure, microwave butter on 100% (HIGH) 30 seconds or until melted. Stir in flour. Microwave on 100% (HIGH) 30 seconds. Stir in milk. Microwave on 100% (HIGH) 3 to 4 minutes or until mixture comes to a boil and starts to thicken, stirring once. Stir in cheese, salt, pepper, dry mustard and nutmeg. Drain cabbage. Stir sauce into cabbage. If necessary, microwave on 100% (HIGH) 2 minutes to reheat. Makes 4 servings.

Squash with Pepita Nuts

Chayote con Pepitas — *Mexico*

Chayote squash is sometimes hard to find. If not available, substitute three medium-size zucchini squash. Sunflower seeds can be used if you can't find pepitas.

3 medium-size Chayote squash
1/3 cup coarsely chopped pepitas
1/4 cup butter or margarine

Peel squash, remove seeds and cut in 1-inch cubes. Place pepitas and butter in a medium-size microwave-safe bowl. Microwave on 100% (HIGH) 2 to 3 minutes or until seeds are toasted. Stir in squash. Cover tightly. Microwave on 100% (HIGH) 4 to 6 minutes or until squash is tender. Makes 4 servings.

Sauerkraut Casserole

U. S. A.

The ingredients in this recipe are typical of the Midwest, but if you search back you might find this recipe has some German relatives. This would taste great served with pork roast.

4 slices bacon
1 medium-size onion, chopped
2 medium-size cooking apples, peeled, cored, chopped
1 (32-oz.) jar sauerkraut, drained, well rinsed
1/2 cup chicken broth
1/4 cup dry Vermouth
2 tablespoons soft light-brown sugar
1/2 teaspoon caraway seeds
1/4 teaspoon black pepper

Lay bacon in large microwave-safe casserole dish. Cover with a paper towel. Microwave on 100% (HIGH) 4 minutes or until crisp. Drain bacon on a paper towel, crumble and set aside. Stir onion and apple into bacon fat. Cover tightly. Microwave on 100% (HIGH) 4 to 5 minutes or until tender. Stir in sauerkraut, chicken broth, Vermouth, brown sugar, caraway seeds and pepper. Re-cover and microwave on 100% (HIGH) 8 to 10 minutes or until heated through, stirring once during cooking. Makes 4 to 5 servings.

Leeks Au Gratin

Poireaux au Gratin — *France*

Leeks are a member of the onion family, in fact they look like giant green onions. They have a very delicate flavor. If the leeks are small and tender, you can use the whole piece. Unfortunately, most leeks sold in the supermarkets are very large and the outside stems are quite tough.

6 small tender leeks, cleaned, ends trimmed
2 tablespoons butter or margarine
2 tablespoons all-purpose flour
1 cup milk
1 chicken bouillon cube
1/2 cup Gruyére cheese
Pinch of nutmeg
2 tablespoons freshly grated Parmesan cheese
1/4 teaspoon paprika

Place leeks in a medium-size rectangular microwave-safe casserole dish. Cover tightly. Microwave on 100% (HIGH) 6 to 8 minutes or until tender. Let stand, covered, 5 minutes. To prepare sauce, in a 2-cup glass measure, microwave butter on 100% (HIGH) 15 to 20 seconds or until melted. Stir in flour. Microwave on 100% (HIGH) 30 seconds. Whisk in milk, add bouillon cube. Microwave on 100% (HIGH) 3 to 5 minutes or until mixture thickens. Stir in cheese and nutmeg. Shape leeks in coils by holding white end and wrapping leek around. Secure with a wooden pick, if necessary. Wash casserole dish. Place leek coils in dry casserole dish. Pour sauce over top. Sprinkle with Parmesan cheese and paprika. Cover tightly. Microwave on 100% (HIGH) 2 to 3 minutes or until hot. Makes 6 servings.

Corn Pudding

Atole — *Mexico*

This is a spoonable pudding that doesn't have to be baked.

1-1/2 cups whipping cream
2 tablespoons butter or margarine
1/3 cup yellow cornmeal
1 (10-oz.) pkg. frozen corn or 1-1/2 cups fresh corn
2 tablespoons chopped pimentos
2 tablespoons chopped mild green chilies

Place cream and butter in a large microwave-safe bowl. Microwave on 100% (HIGH) 5 minutes or until cream comes to a boil, stirring once during cooking. Stir in cornmeal. Microwave on 100% (HIGH) 4 to 6 minutes or until mixture thickens, stirring once during cooking. Stir in corn. Microwave on 100% (HIGH) 5 minutes or until corn is tender, stirring once during cooking. Stir in pimento and chilies. Makes 4 to 6 servings.

Stuffed Apples in Apple Brandy

Gefullte Apfeln in Apfel Weinbrand — *Germany*

Roasted apples are as popular in Germany as they are in England. This version could really come from either country. Serve these apples as an accompaniment to baked ham.

1/4 cup dark raisins or dried currants
3/4 cup apple brandy
1 cup fresh cranberries
1/4 cup light-brown sugar
1/8 teaspoon ground cinnamon
Pinch of nutmeg
4 cooking apples

In a small bowl, combine raisins and 1/4 cup of apple brandy. Let stand 15 minutes. Mix in cranberries, brown sugar and nutmeg. Cut a 1/2-inch slice from top of each apple. Remove core, making a 1-inch column down center. Place apples in a medium-size microwave-safe dish. Spoon cranberry mixture evenly into each hollow apple. Pour remaining apple brandy over apples. Cover tightly. Microwave on 100% (HIGH) 5 minutes. Turn each apple a half turn. Re-cover and microwave on 100% (HIGH) 5 minutes more or until apples are tender. Let stand, covered, 10 minutes. Makes 4 servings

Bulgar Pilaf

Pilav — *Turkey*

Bulgar is frequently used in Middle Eastern cooking in the same way rice would be used. Bulgar is whole-wheat that has been cooked, dried and cracked in small pieces. The taste is similar to brown rice.

2 tablespoons butter or margarine
1/2 medium-size onion, chopped
1 cup bulgar
1-1/2 cups chicken broth
1/4 cup minced fresh parsley

Place butter and onion in a medium-size microwave-safe casserole dish. Microwave on 100% (HIGH) 2 to 3 minutes or until onion is tender. Stir in bulgar. Microwave on 100% (HIGH) 2 minutes. Stir in chicken broth. Cover tightly. Microwave on 100% (HIGH) 8 to 10 minutes or until liquid is absorbed and bulgar is tender. Stir in parsley. Makes 4 servings.

Pilaf

Pilau — *Turkey*

Pilaf is a Middle Eastern staple, as rice is plentiful and economical. This recipe is the classic version, but if you travel in the Middle East you will find a variation for each family.

1/4 cup butter or margarine
1 medium-size onion, chopped
1-1/2 cups uncooked white long-grain rice
3 cups chicken broth
3 tablespoons pine nuts

Place butter and onion in a large microwave-safe casserole dish. Microwave on 100% (HIGH) 2 to 2-1/2 minutes or until onion is tender. Stir in rice. Microwave on 100% (HIGH) 2 to 3 minutes or until rice is very hot. Pour in chicken broth. Cover tightly. Microwave on 100% (HIGH) 15 minutes. Stir and re-cover. Microwave on 50% (MEDIUM) 10 to 12 minutes more or until rice is tender and liquid is absorbed. Place pine nuts on a paper towel in microwave oven. Microwave on 100% (HIGH) 1 minute or until toasted. Stir nuts into pilaf. Makes 4 servings.

Florentine Rice

U. S. A.

Spinach and rice are a flavorful and colorful combination. Anytime you see a recipe called Florentine (in the style of Florence), you know it will have spinach.

2 cups cooked white long-grain rice
1 (10-oz.) pkg. frozen chopped spinach, thawed, well drained
3/4 cup shredded Swiss cheese (3 ozs.)
1/4 teaspoon ground nutmeg
1/2 cup milk
1 egg, beaten

In a medium-size bowl, mix all ingredients until well blended. Spoon into a 1-quart microwave-safe dish. Cover tightly. Microwave on 70% (MEDIUM-HIGH) 6 to 8 minutes or until set. Makes 4 servings.

Rice with Chilies

Arroz con Chilies

M e x i c o

Serve this rice with enchiladas or tacos if you want to be authentic. If you love this rice as much as I do, serve it with most anything, regardless of nationality.

1/2 medium-size onion, finely chopped
2 tablespoons butter or margarine
1 (2-oz.) can diced Anaheim chilies
2 tablespoons chopped fresh cilantro
2 cups cooked white long-grain rice
1 (10-oz.) pkg. frozen corn, thawed
3/4 cup dairy sour cream
1 cup shredded Cheddar cheese (4 ozs.)

Place onion and butter in a large microwave-safe bowl. Microwave on 100% (HIGH) 2 minutes or until onion is tender. Stir in chilies, cilantro, rice and corn. Cover tightly. Microwave on 100% (HIGH) 2 to 3 minutes or until hot throughout. Stir. If necessary, microwave on 100% (HIGH) 1 to 2 minutes more. Stir in sour cream and Cheddar cheese. Re-cover and microwave on 100% (HIGH) 2 to 3 minutes or until cheese melts. Makes 4 to 6 servings.

Fettuccine with Tomatoes & Spinach

Fettuccine Pumate

I t a l y

Italian sun-dried tomatoes packed in olive oil have become popular. They are available in speciality markets, or you can dry your own Italian tomatoes and pack them in oil with some fresh basil.

1/4 cup pine nuts
1/4 cup olive oil
1 clove garlic, minced
1/3 cup sun-dried tomatoes with oil, choppped
1 bunch fresh spinach, washed, stems removed
8-ozs. fettuccine, cooked, drained
1/3 cup freshly grated Parmesan cheese

Place pine nuts on a paper towel in microwave oven. Microwave on 100% (HIGH) 2 to 2-1/2 minutes or until toasted. Set aside. In a large microwave-safe bowl, combine olive oil and garlic. Microwave on 100% (HIGH) 1 to 2 minutes or until oil is flavored with garlic. Stir in tomatoes and spinach. Cover tightly. Microwave on 100% (HIGH) 3 to 3-1/2 minutes or until spinach is wilted. Add hot fettuccine and 1/4 cup of Parmesan cheese. Toss together. Top with pine nuts and remaining Parmesan cheese. Makes 4 servings.

Fancy desserts bring to mind French chefs creating masterpieces that take hours to prepare. On the opposite end of the spectrum, when you think of Chinese food you are hard pressed to think of a dessert. In the middle of the cuisine spectrum falls American desserts. To me these are the best! There is nothing more satisfying than a chocolate fudge cake or a fresh berry cobbler. They are a perfect ending to any meal regardless of nationality. The early French chefs did create or refine many of the basic techniques for desserts though, cream filled pastries, fruit tarts and *gateaux* are usually purchased from a bakery or *patissere* for special occasion meals. For an everyday dinner you will find an assortment of cheeses and fresh fruit to be the preferred dessert in many European countries. Or even something as simple as a good strong cup of espresso or coffee is often served.

A tender, flaky pastry for tarts or pies is an art appreciated in all countries. Even the Chinese serve a custard-filled tart with a multi-layered pastry. I recommend cooking the pastry unfilled first either in the microwave or the conventional oven. When done correctly the results are similar.

Egg-based cooked soufflés are very continental, but alas do not hold their regal height well when cooked in a microwave oven due to the moist method of microwave cooking. Try instead a cold gelatin based soufflé for beautiful height and taste. Egg-based custards or custard sauces like a *crème anglaise* can be successfully cooked in the microwave oven, but they do require a lower cooking power to prevent overcooking. The results of an overcooked egg custard are easy to spot—a tough texture with the interior full of air holes and lots of liquid that weeps out into the dish. A Mexican *flan,* which is an egg custard with caramel coating, can be done beautifully and quickly in the microwave oven and *flan* is a perfect light ending to the Mexican *cena* (dinner).

Following the historical path of spices can really be enlightning. For example, ginger seems to have originated in the Orient, appearing mostly in savory dishes. But gingerbread, usually considered an early American favorite, was eaten in ancient Egypt. Queen Elizabeth I had a baker in her kitchen whose sole job was to create gingerbread portraits of her court. This English concoction explains the popularity of gingerbread in early America. Even Peter the Great of Russia was given huge gingerbread cakes upon his birth.

Pots of Cream with Chocolate

Pots de Creme au Chocolat *France*

The original pots de creme *recipe is an extra rich custard served in small individual cups. The addition of* au chocolat *makes this a dense, rich chocolate-like mousse dessert.*

6 ozs. semisweet chocolate bits
1/2 cup whipping cream
2 tablespoons sugar
2 egg yolks, beaten
1 teaspoon vanilla extract
Whipped cream, if desired

In a medium-size microwave-safe bowl, combine chocolate bits, whipping cream and sugar. Microwave on 100% (HIGH) 1 minute. Stir well. Microwave on 100% (HIGH) 1 minute more. Stir again. Microwave on 100% (HIGH) in 30 second increments until chocolate is melted. Stir until mixture is very smooth. In a medium-size bowl, beat chocolate mixture into egg yolks until smooth. Stir in vanilla. Pour into 1/2-cup pots. Top with dollops of whipped cream, if desired. Makes 4 servings.

Wine Custard

Zabaglione *Italy*

Zabaglione *in Italy,* sabayon *in France and* weinschaum *in Germany are all the same light custard, but made with different wines ranging from Marsala to Madiera to a sweet white Moselle. The key to making this custard is constant whisking to prevent lumps and add lightness.*

6 egg yolks
1/3 cup sugar
1/2 cup Marsala or Madiera wine

In a medium-size microwave-safe bowl, whisk egg yolks and sugar until very light in color. Stir in wine. Microwave on 70% (MEDIUM-HIGH) 1 to 1-1/2 minutes, whisking every 15 seconds. If eggs curdle, immediately strain through a fine sieve or process in a food processor fitted with a metal blade. Pour into 6 dessert dishes. Makes 6 servings.

Coffee Charlotte

English

The English love their desserts. They usually serve more than one at a time, using a small trolley to wheel them out. Even though tea is the national drink, they like coffee-flavored desserts.

1 (3-oz.) pkg. ladyfingers (about 8 to 12)
3 tablespoons brandy
1-1/2 cups whipping cream
1/2 teaspoon vanilla extract
1 tablespoon instant coffee granules
1 tablespoon water
3/4 cup butter or margarine
1/2 cup powdered sugar
2 eggs

Cut ladyfingers in half lengthwise and sprinkle cut surfaces with brandy. In a medium-size glass dish, stand ladyfingers up around inside, cut side toward center of bowl. In a medium-size bowl, whip cream and vanilla until soft peaks form. In a 1-cup measure, combine coffee granules and water. Microwave on 100% (HIGH) 10 seconds. In a small bowl, cream butter and powdered sugar, then beat in eggs and coffee. Fold egg mixture into whipped cream until smoooth. Pour into ladyfinger-lined dish. If desired, garnish top with any remaining ladyfingers. Refrigerate until ready to serve. Makes 6 servings.

Cooking Tip:

To quickly blanch almonds, bring one cup of water to a boil. Remove from microwave and drop in almonds. Let stand for one minute, then drain. Skins will easily slip off.

Grand Marnier Flavored Sweet Omelet

Omelets Soufflé au Grand Marnier *France*

Sweet omelets are an unfamiliar taste to many Americans. But once you've tried one, you'll want to experiment with other fruit liqueurs or brandies.

2 eggs, separated
2 tablespoons sugar
1 tablespoon grated orange peel
1 tablespoon Grand Marnier liqueur
1 tablespoon powdered sugar

In a medium-size bowl, whip egg whites until stiff but not dry. In a small bowl, beat egg yolks, sugar, orange peel and liqueur. Gently fold yolk mixture into stiff egg whites. Pour into an 8-inch round microwave-safe glass cake dish. Microwave on 100% (HIGH) 2 to 2-1/2 minutes or until mixture is dry on top. Remove omelet to a serving dish. Fold in half and sprinkle with powdered sugar. Makes 2 servings.

Cold Pumpkin Soufflé

U. S. A.

The pumpkin has been associated with our American heritage as far back as the pilgrims, especially around Thanksgiving. This updated recipe using pumpkin will be popular all year long.

2 (.25-oz.) envelopes unflavored gelatin
1/4 cup water
4 eggs, separated
1 cup whipping cream
3/4 cup sugar
1 (1-lb.) can pumpkin
1 teaspoon pumpkin pie spice
Whipped cream and edible flowers to decorate

In a small microwave-safe bowl, sprinkle gelatin over water. Let stand until gelatin is soft. Microwave on 100% (HIGH) 1 minute. Stir until gelatin dissolves. In a medium-size bowl, beat egg whites until stiff but not dry. In another medium-size bowl, beat whipping cream until soft peaks form. In a large bowl, beat egg yolks and sugar until thick and light yellow in color. Stir in gelatin. Beat in pumpkin and pumpkin pie spice. Fold in egg whites, then whipped cream. Spoon soufflé into a soufflé dish. Refrigerate until ready to serve. Decorate with whipped cream and edible flowers. Makes 6 servings.

 Cold Pumpkin Soufflé, above.

Bread Pudding

U. S. A.

Bread pudding is such a homey, comforting dessert. It seems to have been an early American way to use up stale bread. In the southern states, it is served with a whiskey sauce as is this recipe. It's great plain or served with Light Custard Sauce, page 55, instead of Whiskey Sauce.

8 slices white, whole-wheat or raisin bread, crusts removed, cut in cubes
1/2 cup dark raisins
2 cups milk
2 eggs, beaten
1/3 cup sugar
1/2 teaspoon ground cinnamon
1 teaspoon vanilla extract

Whiskey Sauce:
1/2 cup sugar
1 tablespoon cornstarch
2 to 3 tablespoons bourbon whiskey
1/4 cup butter or margarine
1 cup whipping cream
1/2 teaspoon vanilla extract

Prepare Whiskey Sauce. In a 9-inch round microwave-safe cake dish, combine bread cubes and raisins. In a medium-size microwave-safe bowl, microwave milk on 100% (HIGH) 5 minutes or just until milk boils. Whisk in eggs, sugar, cinnamon and vanilla. Pour over bread cubes and raisins. Set dish on an inverted microwave-safe saucer in microwave oven. Microwave on 100% (HIGH) 8 to 9 minutes or until liquid has set. Let stand 20 minutes. Serve with Whiskey Sauce. Makes 6 servings.

Whiskey Sauce:
In a small microwave-safe bowl, combine sugar, cornstarch and whiskey. Add butter. Microwave on 100% (HIGH) 1 to 1-1/2 minutes or until butter is melted. Whisk in cream. Microwave on 100% (HIGH) 3 to 5 minutes or until mixture begins to thicken. Stir in vanilla. Makes 1-1/4 cups.

Rum Rice Pudding

U. S. A.

Rice pudding lovers usually have definite preferences as to what rice pudding should contain. Some like raisins, others prefer candied fruit and purists insist on only a dusting of cinnamon or nutmeg. Use this recipe as is or include your favorite combinations!

1/2 cup uncooked white rice
1 cup hot water
1/2 cup golden raisins
2 tablespoons rum
1-1/4 cups milk
1/4 teaspoon salt
1/3 cup sugar
2 egg yolks
1 cup half and half
1/2 (.25-oz.) pkg. unflavored gelatin
1 teaspoon vanilla extract

In a large microwave-safe bowl, cover rice with hot water. Let stand 15 minutes, then drain thoroughly. Return rice to bowl. Meanwhile, in a small bowl, soak raisins in rum. Combine drained rice with milk and salt. Microwave on 100% (HIGH) 15 minutes, stirring 3 times during cooking. In a medium-size microwave-safe bowl, combine sugar and egg yolks. Stir in half and half. Microwave on 100% (HIGH) 3 minutes or until mixture begins to thicken, stirring well every minute. Stir in gelatin until dissolved. Combine rice with raisins and rum, egg mixture and vanilla. Pour into a serving dish. Refrigerate until chilled, stirring after 20 minutes. Makes 4 servings.

Custard with Brown Sugar Topping

Crème Brûlée

France

This wonderfully rich cream custard is topped with a thin layer of brown sugar and briefly placed under a broiler to form a thin crust. This is a very thin custard, so don't be surprised at its consistency.

2 cups whipping cream
4 egg yolks
1/4 cup sugar
1 teaspoon vanilla extract
1/4 cup plus 2 tablespoons light-brown sugar

In a medium-size microwave-safe bowl, microwave whipping cream on 100% (HIGH) 6 minutes or just until cream begins to boil. In a food processor fitted with a metal blade or a blender, process egg yolks and sugar just until blended. With machine running, pour in hot cream. Return mixture to bowl. Microwave on 50% (MEDIUM) 10 to 12 minutes or until mixture coats back of a spoon, whisking every 2 minutes. Stir in vanilla. Strain mixture and spoon into 6 individual soufflé dishes. Refrigerate at least 8 hours. Preheat broiler. Sift 1 tablespoon of brown sugar evenly over top of each custard. Broil under preheated broiler just until brown sugar melts, watching very carefully during cooking. Makes 6 servings.

Fresh Fruit Salad With Cream

Macedoine de Fruits — *France & England*

I first tasted this fresh fruit compote in a French restaurant. What made me remember it was the lovely citrus-flavored sugar syrup with which the fruit was mixed. I later saw a similar English recipe, but made with sherry and whipped cream. This recipe is a combination of the two, making it now an American recipe!

1/2 cup sugar
1 cup water
Peel 1/2 orange, finely chopped
Peel 1/2 lemon, finely chopped
1/2 medium-size cantalope
2 medium-size bananas
2 medium-size oranges
1 medium-size pear
1 medium-size apple
3/4 cup seedless grapes
2 tablespoons sherry
2 cups whipping cream

In a medium-size microwave-safe bowl, combine sugar, water and orange and lemon peels. Microwave on 100% (HIGH) 2 to 4 minutes or until syrup comes to a boil, then microwave 5 minutes more. Let stand until room temperature. Strain out peel. Peel and cut cantalope, bananas, oranges, pear and apple into bite-size pieces. In a serving bowl, toss all fruit with syrup and sherry. Refrigerate until ready to serve. Serve with cream to pour over individual servings. Makes 4 to 6 servings.

Cooking Tip:
Use paper towels for a quick, easy clean-up plate when reheating nonliquid foods.

Pastry Crust

U. S. A.

The key to a good pie crust is to not overmix it or overcook it in the microwave oven. This pasty makes a nine-inch pie shell.

1 cup all-purpose flour
1/4 cup vegetable shortening
1/8 teaspoon salt
2 to 3 tablespoons cold water

In a small bowl, combine flour and shortening. Using a fork, blend until mixture is about size of peas. Add 2 tablespoons of cold water. Stir or use hands to blend completely until dough holds together. If needed, add more cold water. When dough is smooth, shape in a ball, then flatten slightly. Roll out to a 12-inch circle on a floured surface or between 2 sheets of waxed paper. Gently transfer dough into a 9-inch microwave-safe pie plate. Crimp edges and trim. Using a fork, prick bottom and sides several times. Microwave on 100% (HIGH) 3 minutes. Rotate dish one-half turn. Microwave on 100% (HIGH) 1 to 2 minutes more or until crust is dry looking, watching carefully during cooking. Makes 1 (9-inch) pie crust.

Lemon Sour Cream Pie

U. S. A.

Lemon is such a palate cleansing flavor that this pie can be served after any meal, regardless of the nationality of the meal.

1 cup sugar
3-1/2 tablespoons cornstarch
1 cup milk
3 egg yolks, beaten
2 tablespoons butter or margarine
1-1/2 teaspoons finely grated lemon peel
1/3 cup fresh lemon juice
1 cup dairy sour cream
1 (8-inch) baked pie shell
1 cup whipping cream
1/2 teaspoon vanilla extract
1/4 cup powdered sugar

In a large microwave-safe bowl, combine sugar and cornstarch. Stir in milk. Microwave on 100% (HIGH) 3 to 4 minutes or until mixture begins to boil, then microwave 2 to 3 minutes more or until mixture thickens. In a small bowl, pour about 1/4 cup of hot mixture into beaten egg yolks. Whisk quickly to combine. Pour egg mixture back into milk mixture. Whisk to thoroughly mix. Microwave on 50% (MEDIUM) 2 minutes, stirring twice during cooking. Stir in butter and lemon peel and juice. Let stand until room temperature. Stir in sour cream. Pour into pie shell. In a small bowl, whip cream, vanilla and powdered sugar until stiff peaks form. Spread over filling. Makes 6 to 8 servings.

Orange Glazed Pears

U. S. A.

Stewed fruits are an historical American favorite. Spring, summer or autumn—fresh pears are readily available. To serve, tuck a small mint leaf in with the stem for a pretty garnish.

3 cups water
3/4 cup sugar
3 whole cloves
2 (2-inch) pieces cinnamon
4 medium-size pears
1/4 cup fresh lemon juice
1 teaspoon vanilla extract
1 (16-oz.) can apricot halves, drained, cut in half
3/4 cup orange marmalade
2 tablespoons orange liqueur
Fresh mint leaves to garnish

In a 2-quart microwave-safe soufflé dish, combine water, sugar, cloves and cinnamon. Microwave on 100% (HIGH) 8 to 10 minutes or until syrup boils. Peel pears, leaving stems on, and brush with lemon juice. Stir vanilla into syrup. Place pears in syrup. If necessary, lay pears on their sides to cover with syrup. Cover tightly. Microwave on 70% (MEDIUM-HIGH) 8 to 10 minutes or until pears are completely cooked and tender. Add apricots. Re-cover and let stand until room temperature. To prepare sauce, in a small microwave-safe bowl, combine 1/2 cup of syrup, marmalade and liqueur. Microwave on 100% (HIGH) 3 to 4 minutes or until hot. Place pears and apricots in 4 individual dessert dishes. Spoon sauce over pears. Garnish with mint leaves. Makes 4 servings.

Marinated Apricots & Figs, page 15; Orange Glazed Pears, above.

Rhubarb-Strawberry Crumble

U. S. A.

Rhubarb was originally called pie plant because of its sharp flavor. About all you could do with it was mix it with sugar and bake it in a pie! Rhubarb paired with strawberries makes a mild but zingy combination.

1-1/2 cups (1/2-inch-thick-slices) fresh rhubarb or 1 (16-oz.) bag frozen rhubarb, thawed

2 cups strawberries, stems removed, cut in slices

1 cup sugar

1/2 cup all-purpose flour

3/4 cup dark-brown sugar

1/2 cup regular oats

1/2 teaspoon ground cinnamon

1/4 teaspoon ground nutmeg

1/2 cup butter or margarine

In a large bowl, combine rhubarb, strawberries and sugar. Spoon into an 8-inch round microwave-safe cake dish. In a medium-size bowl, blend flour, brown sugar, oats, cinnamon, nutmeg and butter. Crumble evenly over rhubarb and strawberries. Microwave on 100% (HIGH) 5 minutes. Rotate dish one-half turn. Microwave on 100% (HIGH) 5 to 6 minutes more or until rhubarb is tender and edges are bubbling. Makes 6 to 8 servings.

Toasted Almond Powder

Praline *France*

This sweet powder can be used to sprinkle on a fresh fruit compote or added to whipped cream for flavoring. It's great as a topping for ice cream.

2 ozs. blanched almonds (see Cooking Tip, page 137)

1/4 cup sugar

2 tablespoons water

Grease a baking sheet. Spread almonds on a microwave-safe plate. Microwave on 100% (HIGH) 3 to 4 minutes or until toasted. In a medium-size microwave-safe glass or ceramic bowl, combine sugar and water. Microwave on 100% (HIGH) 5 to 6 minutes or just until sugar begins to brown. Stir in hot nuts. Spread on greased baking sheet. Cool completely and break in small pieces. In a food processor fitted with a metal blade, process praline pieces until very fine. Makes 1/2 cup.

Strawberry Fool

England

This type of fool is a sweetened fruit mixture combined with whipped cream. Any fruit works great—apricots, blackberries or peaches for example. If fresh fruit is not available, use unsweetened frozen fruit.

2 cups fresh strawberries, hulled, cut in half
1/3 cup sugar
1/2 teaspoon vanilla extract
1-1/2 cups whipping cream

In a medium-size microwave-safe bowl, combine strawberries and sugar. Cover tightly. Microwave on 100% (HIGH) 5 to 8 minutes or until berries are softened and sugar dissolves in juice. Stir in vanilla. Let stand until room temperature. Thirty minutes before serving, in a medium-size bowl, whip cream until soft peaks form. Gently fold in berry mixture, leaving a swirled effect. Refrigerate until ready to serve. Makes 4 to 6 servings.

Orange Ice

Granita Arancia

Italy

Use this recipe as a base for other fruit juice flavors—grape or guava juice tastes great.

1/2 cup sugar
1/2 cup water
3-1/2 cups fresh orange juice
1 tablespoon finely grated orange peel
Orange shell halves

In a large microwave-safe bowl, combine sugar and water. Microwave on 100% (HIGH) 1 to 2 minutes or until water boils. Stir until sugar is completely dissolved. Let stand until room temperature. Stir in orange juice and peel. Pour into an ice cream freezer and freeze according to manufacturer's directions. Or pour into ice trays and freeze until firm, stirring frequently. To serve, mound into orange shell halves. Makes 3 pints.

Lemon Ice

Granita Lemon — *Italy*

Lemon ice served in lemon shells is a favorite dessert or afternoon snack in Italy.

1-1/2 cups sugar
4 cups water
1 cup fresh lemon juice
1 tablespoon finely grated lemon peel
Lemon shell halves

In a large microwave-safe bowl, combine sugar and water. Microwave on 100% (HIGH) 10 to 12 minutes or until water begins to boil. Stir until sugar is completely dissolved. Let stand until room temperature. Mix in lemon juice and peel. Pour into an ice cream freezer and freeze according to manufacturer's directions. Or pour into freezer trays and freeze until firm, stirring frequently. To serve, mound into lemon shell halves. Makes 3 pints.

Strawberry Sorbet

Fraises Sorbet — *France*

Sorbet is similar to what we call sherbet, but is usually made with fruit, sugar and flavorings, no dairy products at all. Sorbet is really frozen fruit ice. Using frozen fruit makes this easy to prepare all year long.

1 (.25-oz.) envelope unflavored gelatin
1 cup water
2 (10-oz.) pkgs. frozen strawberries
1/2 cup corn syrup
1/4 cup orange liqueur
2 tablespoons lemon juice

Place a large bowl in freezer to chill. In a small microwave-safe bowl, sprinkle gelatin over water. Let stand 5 minutes or until gelatin is soft. Microwave on 100% (HIGH) 3 minutes or just until water boils. Stir until gelatin is completely dissolved. In a food processor fitted with a metal blade or a blender, process strawberries and juice to a puree. In a large bowl, combine gelatin mixture, pureed fruit, corn syrup, liqueur and lemon juice. Pour mixture into a 9'' x 9'' square dish. Place in freezer about 3 hours, stirring occasionally to keep mixture partially frozen. Spoon partially frozen mixture into chilled bowl. Beat with an electric mixer until smooth but still frozen. Refreeze 2 to 3 hours before serving. Makes 6 to 8 servings.

Breakfast & Brunch

European, South American and Scandinavian countries take their first meal of the day very seriously. Starting off with a cup of good coffee and perhaps some sweet bread, they follow a little later with a heartier breakfast meal. A favorite breakfast dish in Japan is *miso* soup with tofu or vegetables added for their nutritional value.

Americans still love their traditional eggs and bacon with pancakes or waffles occasionally. If my family is an example though, cold cereal and toast seem to be the norm as mornings get busier. In Mexico a *tortilla* takes the place of American toast. *Tortillas* are very flat rounds like pancakes made from corn or wheat flour.

The Spanish use the word *tortilla*, but they are referring to an egg omelet served either flat and round or rolled French-style. The Spanish *tortillas* or omelets are served not just for breakfast but as a meal by themselves at the midday meal or as an appetizer or first course. For an appetizer the omelet would be cut into wedges and eaten with the salad. For a heartier meal, several omelets would be cooked then stacked with vegetables and/or meat fillings in between, then cut into wedges and served like a *torte*.

The Chinese use eggs primarily as a binder for other ingredients. *Egg foo young* starts with a scrambled egg base to which chopped fresh vegetables and/or meat are mixed in. This mixture is then fried like a pancake. Sometimes a scrambled egg mixture is cooked like a very thin omelet, then sliced into thin strips and added to soups or other dishes for its color and protein as well as taste.

In France you would find eggs for breakfast only in "Americanized" homes or hotels. They lay claim to inventing the omelet as we know it today, but only serve it or other egg dishes as an appetizer, light lunch or dinner.

Swiss-Style Oatmeal

Museli Switzerland

Americans tend to cook their hot cereal straight out of the box without giving much creative thought to it. In Europe where hearty breakfast cereal is a treat, you will find fruit, nuts and honey added. If you only need a single serving, use one-fourth of this recipe and prepare it right in your cereal bowl.

2-1/2 cups water
1/2 cup assorted dried fruits (raisins, apricots, apples, dates, prunes), diced
2 tablespoons honey
1-1/4 cups regular oats
1/4 cup chopped pecans
Milk

In a large microwave-safe bowl, combine water and dried fruits. Microwave on 100% (HIGH) 6 to 8 minutes or until water begins to boil. Stir in honey and oats. Microwave on 50% (MEDIUM) 2 minutes. Stir. Let stand 5 minutes. Spoon into 4 cereal bowls. Sprinkle with pecans and serve with milk. Makes 4 servings.

Eggs Cooked in Bread with Ham & Cheese

Oeufs Sur Canapes France

This recipe reminded me of the American "Hole in One" recipe where the egg is cooked in a hole in a slice of bread. The French always seem to take a simple idea and make it special. Gruyére cheese is similar to our Swiss cheese.

1 (3- x 5-inch) slice French bread, 1/2-inch thick
1 tablespoon butter or margarine
1 egg
1 tablespoon finely chopped cooked ham
2 tablespoons shredded Gruyére cheese

Gently scoop out a hole in side of bread about size of an egg yolk. Place butter in a flat microwave-safe plate. Microwave on 100% (HIGH) 30 seconds or until melted. Place bread, hole side up, on top of melted butter. Gently break egg into hole in bread. Pierce yolk with a fork. Sprinkle ham on egg and bread, then sprinkle with cheese. Microwave on 70% (MEDIUM-HIGH) 1 to 2 minutes or until white of egg is set and cheese melts. Makes 1 serving.

Clockwise from top: Apple Butter, page 156; Strawberry-Apricot Jam, page 156; Swiss-Style Oatmeal, above.

Ham & Vegetable Omelette

Piperade con Jamon — *Spain*

This Basque dish is similar to pisto, *an omelet mixed with onions, bell peppers, vegetables and sometimes meat. It is known in America as a western omelet and probably was introduced here by Basque immigrants.*

2 tablespoon olive oil
2 medium-size tomatoes, seeds removed, finely chopped
1 medium-size onion, finely chopped
1 red bell pepper, seeded, thinly sliced
8 ozs. cooked ham, diced
1 cup chopped fresh spinach
4 eggs
2 tablespoons water

Combine olive oil, tomatoes, onion and bell pepper in an 8- or 9-inch round microwave-safe cake dish. Cover tightly. Microwave on 100% (HIGH) 5 to 6 minutes or until vegetables are soft. Stir in ham and spinach. Re-cover and microwave on 100% (HIGH) 2 minutes. In a small bowl, beat eggs and water. Pour over vegetable mixture. Microwave on 100% (HIGH) 2 minutes. Gently stir, bringing cooked outer edges to center. Microwave on 100% (HIGH) in 1 minute segments, repeating stirring procedure until eggs are just set and still slightly moist. Cut in wedges to serve. Makes 4 servings.

Hangtown Fry

U. S. A.

Legend has it that this dish originated in Placerville, California, also known in the Gold Rush Days as Hangtown. A miner about to be hung was granted a last wish for his favorite dish, scrambled eggs with Olympia oysters. In the two days it took to go to Washington for the oysters, the miner escaped!

4 slices bacon
12 Olympia oysters or 6 regular oysters, shucked
2 tablespoons butter or margarine
3 eggs
2 tablespoons water

Lay bacon slices flat in an 8-inch round microwave-safe cake dish. Cover with a paper towel. Microwave on 100% (HIGH) 4 to 6 minutes or until crisp. Drain bacon on a paper towel, crumble and set aside. Drain off fat from dish. Place oysters in dish. Pierce each with a fork. Dot with butter. Cover tightly. Microwave on 100% (HIGH) 1 minute. In a small bowl, beat eggs and water. Pour over oysters. Sprinkle crumbled bacon over egg mixture. Microwave on 100% (HIGH) 1-1/2 minutes. Gently stir, bringing cooked outer edges to center. Microwave on 100% (HIGH) 1 to 2 minutes more or until eggs are set but still moist. Slide cooked mixture onto a serving plate. Fold over omelet-style or serve flat. Makes 2 servings.

Baked Eggs in Cheese

Gebakken Eieren en Kaas — *Holland*

So many European dishes are considered "Continental" that it is difficult to associate them with a specific country. This dish uses Edam cheese which is native to Holland. This is delicious served on toasted English muffin halves.

1-1/4 cups shredded Edam cheese (5 ozs.)

6 eggs

2 tablespoons sliced green onion, stem included

1/2 cup whipping cream

Grease an 8-inch round microwave-safe cake dish. Sprinkle 1/2 of cheese evenly over bottom of dish. Make 6 (1-inch) evenly spaced round indentations in cheese. Break 1 egg into each indentation. Pierce yolks with a fork. Sprinkle green onions and remaining cheese over eggs. Pour cream over all. Cover tightly. Microwave on 70% (MEDIUM-HIGH) 5 minutes. Turn dish a half turn. Microwave on 70% (MEDIUM-HIGH) 1 to 2 minutes more or until eggs are just set. Makes 6 servings.

Joe's Special

U. S. A.

This tasty combination originated in San Francisco. While the herbs and flavoring combinations differ, it always contains eggs, ground beef and spinach.

3/4 lb. ground beef

1/2 medium-size onion, diced

1 bunch fresh spinach, washed, stems removed, chopped, or 1 (10-oz.) pkg. frozen spinach, drained well, chopped

1/4 cup dry white wine

1/4 teaspoon dried leaf marjoram, crushed

1/4 teaspoon dried leaf oregano

Salt and black pepper to taste

4 eggs, beaten

Crumble ground beef in a flat microwave-safe casserole dish. Sprinkle with onion. Cover with plastic wrap. Microwave on 100% (HIGH) 3 minutes. Stir to break meat in small pieces. Re-cover and microwave on 100% (HIGH) 2 to 3 minutes more or until meat is no longer pink. Stir in spinach, wine, marjoram and oregano. Cover tightly. Microwave on 100% (HIGH) 2 minutes or until spinach is heated. Season with salt and pepper. Stir in eggs. Microwave on 100% (HIGH) 3 to 4 minutes or until eggs are just set, stirring twice during cooking. Makes 4 servings.

Scrambled Eggs with Chili

Shakshooka — *Israel*

This spicy version of scrambled eggs was brought to Israel from North Africa where hot spicy food is the norm.

1 (14-1/2-oz.) can whole tomatoes, drained

1 teaspoon chili powder

4 eggs, slightly beaten

Remove seeds from tomatoes and chop finely. In a medium-size microwave-safe dish, combine tomatoes and chili powder. Microwave on 100% (HIGH) 3 minutes. Stir in eggs. Microwave on 100% (HIGH) 2 minutes. Gently stir, bringing cooked outer edges to center. Microwave on 100% (HIGH) 2 minutes more. Stir again, bringing cooked outer edges to center. If eggs are not completely set, microwave on 100% (HIGH) 1 to 2 minutes more. Eggs should still be slightly moist. Makes 4 servings.

Catalan Style Omelet

Tortilla Catalan — *Spain*

In Mexico a tortilla is a flat corn or flour pancake. In Spain a tortilla is an omelet.

1 medium-size onion, finely chopped

2 tablespoons olive oil

4 eggs, beaten

In an 8-inch round microwave-safe cake dish, combine onion and olive oil. Microwave on 100% (HIGH) 2 minutes. Stir. If onions are not translucent, microwave on 100% (HIGH) 1 to 2 minutes more. Stir in eggs. Microwave on 100% (HIGH) 2 minutes. Gently stir, bringing cooked outer edges to center. Microwave on 100% (HIGH) 1 to 2 minutes more or until omelet is puffy and just moist on top. Cut in 3 or 4 wedges to serve. Makes 3 to 4 servings.

Poached Eggs on Spinach

Oeuff au Vin — *France*

The French rarely serve eggs for breakfast, but as a first course or a light midday meal. This would be great for brunch or a light dinner.

2 bunches fresh spinach, washed, stems removed
1/4 cup butter or margarine
1 clove garlic
1 tablespoon all-purpose flour
1 cup whipping cream
2 tablespoons fresh lemon juice
1/8 teaspoon salt
2 cups dry white wine
1 cup water
4 eggs
Paprika

Place spinach in a large microwave-safe bowl. Cover tightly. Microwave on 100% (HIGH) 4 to 6 minutes or until limp. Set aside; do not uncover. To prepare sauce, place butter and garlic in a small microwave-safe bowl. Microwave on 100% (HIGH) 1 to 2 minutes or until butter is melted. Remove garlic and stir in flour. Microwave on 100% (HIGH) 30 seconds. Stir in cream. Microwave on 100% (HIGH) 3 to 5 minutes or until cream starts to thicken. Stir in lemon juice and salt. Set aside. Combine wine and water in a flat 9-inch microwave-safe dish. Microwave on 100% (HIGH) 10 to 12 minutes or until water comes to a full boil. Break eggs into boiling liquid. Pierce yolks with a fork. Microwave on 100% (HIGH) 2 to 3 minutes or until eggs are set. Divide spinach among 4 individual ramkins. Remove eggs from liquid with a slotted spoon and place in center of spinach. Pour sauce over top of each. Sprinkle with paprika. Makes 4 servings.

Chicken Livers Oriental

U. S. A.

Serve this dish with scrambled eggs and coffee cake for an easy, different brunch idea.

1 lb. chicken livers, cut in half
2 tablespoons butter or margarine
1 tablespoon soy sauce
2 tablespoons dry sherry
1 tablespoon all-purpose flour
1 cup whipping cream
1/2 lb. sugar snap peas, ends removed
1/4 cup water chestnuts, thinly sliced

In a large microwave-safe bowl, combine chicken livers, butter, soy sauce and sherry. Cover tightly. Microwave on 100% (HIGH) 3 to 4 minutes or just until livers are done, stirring after 2 minutes of cooking. Remove livers with a slotted spoon and set aside. Whisk in flour, then cream. Microwave on 100% (HIGH) 3 to 5 minutes or until slightly thickened. Stir in livers, peas and water chestnuts. Microwave on 100% (HIGH) 2 to 3 minutes or until heated. Makes 4 to 6 servings.

Strawberry-Apricot Jam *(Photo on page 151)*

U. S. A.

This jam can be made year round by using frozen strawberries and canned apricots. It's an unlikely but fresh tasting combination.

1 (10-oz.) pkg. frozen strawberries in syrup, thawed
1 (16-oz.) can peeled apricots, drained, pits removed, chopped
2 teaspoons finely grated lemon peel
4 cups sugar
1 (6-oz.) bottle liquid fruit pectin

Sterilize 3 (1-pint) jars and lids. Keep hot until needed. In a large microwave-safe bowl, combine strawberries with syrup, apricots, lemon peel and sugar. Microwave on 100% (HIGH) 5 to 8 minutes or until sugar is dissolved, stirring twice during cooking. Cover tightly. Microwave on 100% (HIGH) 4 to 5 minutes more or until mixture reaches a boil. Microwave on 100% (HIGH) 1 minute more. Skim off foam. Let stand 5 minutes. Stir in pectin. Ladle into hot jars to within 1/4 inch of top. Fill and close 1 jar at a time. Wipe rim of jar with a clean damp cloth. Put lid on jar as manufacturer directs. Process jars in a boiling-water bath 10 minutes. Makes about 3 pints.

Apple Butter *(Photo on page 151)*

U. S. A.

This is a quick but tasty version of an American favorite. To save the preparation time of cooking the apples, I have substituted prepared applesauce.

2 cups chunky applesauce
1/2 cup light-brown sugar
1/2 cup granulated sugar
1 teaspoon ground cinnamon
1/8 teaspoon ground cloves
Finely grated peel 1/2 lemon

Sterilize 2 (1-pint) jars and lids. Keep hot until needed. Combine all ingredients in a large microwave-safe bowl. Microwave on 100% (HIGH) 5 minutes. Stir. Microwave on 100% (HIGH) 5 minutes more. Stir. Pour into hot jars and attach lids. Refrigerate until ready to use. Makes 2 cups.

Cooking Tip:
To make a quick homemade-tasting jam, stir 1 tablespoon of chopped nuts into 1 cup of prepared jam. Microwave on 100% (HIGH) 1 minute.

Metric Chart

Comparison to Metric Measure

When You Know	Symbol	Multiply By	To Find	Symbol
teaspoons	tsp	5.0	milliliters	ml
tablespoons	tbsp	15.0	milliliters	ml
fluid ounces	fl. oz.	30.0	milliliters	ml
cups	c	0.24	liters	l
pints	pt.	0.47	liters	l

When You Know	Symbol	Multiply By	To Find	Symbol
quarts	qt.	0.95	liters	l
ounces	oz.	28.0	grams	g
pounds	lb.	0.45	kilograms	kg
Fahrenheit	F	5/9 (after subtracting 32)	Celsius	C

Liquid Measure to Milliliters

1/4 teaspoon	=	1.25 milliliters
1/2 teaspoon	=	2.5 milliliters
3/4 teaspoon	=	3.75 milliliters
1 teaspoon	=	5.0 milliliters
1-1/4 teaspoons	=	6.25 milliliters
1-1/2 teaspoons	=	7.5 milliliters
1-3/4 teaspoons	=	8.75 milliliters
2 teaspoons	=	10.0 milliliters
1 tablespoon	=	15.0 milliliters
2 tablespoons	=	30.0 milliliters

Fahrenheit to Celsius

F	C
200—205	95
220—225	105
245—250	120
275	135
300—305	150
325--330	165
345—350	175
370—375	190
400—405	205
425—430	220
445—450	230
470—475	245
500	260

Liquid Measure to Liters

1/4 cup	=	0.06 liters
1/2 cup	=	0.12 liters
3/4 cup	=	0.18 liters
1 cup	=	0.24 liters
1-1/4 cups	=	0.3 liters
1-1/2 cups	=	0.36 liters
2 cups	=	0.48 liters
2-1/2 cups	=	0.6 liters
3 cups	=	0.72 liters
3-1/2 cups	=	0.84 liters
4 cups	=	0.96 liters
4-1/2 cups	=	1.08 liters
5 cups	=	1.2 liters
5-1/2 cups	=	1.32 liters

POWER LEVEL SETTINGS

Word Designation	Numerical Designation	Power Output at Setting	Percentage of HIGH Setting
HIGH	10	650 watts	100%
MEDIUM HIGH	7	455 watts	70%
MEDIUM	5	325 watts	50%
MEDIUM LOW	3	195 watts	30%
LOW	1	65 watts	10%